ISBN 978-0-9850031-5-9

ISSN 2157-586X

THE JOURNAL OF THE BLACK CATHOLIC THEOLOGICAL SYMPOSIUM (BCTS), was founded in 2007.

MANUSCRIPTS should be submitted to the editorial board by the deadline announced at the Annual Meeting, which is also posted at http://www.bcts.org. All submissions must be formatted in Chicago Turabian style with Works Cited page and sent via electronic mail to Senior Editor, Dr. Kimberly Flint-Hamilton: kflintha@stetson.edu, *and* to Editor, Dr. Cecilia Moore: Cecilia.Moore@notes.udayton.edu. For examples of Chicago Turabian style, see: http://www.press.uchicago.edu/books/turabian/turabian_citationguide.html.

The Journal of the Black Catholic Theological Symposium is composed of original articles by its members and guest contributors, and will not publish manuscripts that have been previously published elsewhere.

REVIEWS of books or films that have relevance to the Black Catholic Theological Symposium may also be submitted and will be considered for publication. Reviews originally published elsewhere will not be considered for publication.

MEMBERSHIP in the Black Catholic Theological Symposium is by invitation only. Those interested in joining the organization may review membership guidelines from Article II of the Constitution, posted on the BCTS web site: http://www.bcts.org, and contact the Secretary of the BCTS, Dr. Shawnee Daniels-Sykes at the following email address: sykess@mtmary.edu.

The opinions expressed in the articles and reviews published in *The Journal of the Black Catholic Theological Symposium* are those of the authors and are not necessarily the opinions of the editorial board, the organization, or the publisher.

The Journal of the Black Catholic Theological Symposium is provided to all paid members of the BCTS. Additional copies of the journal may be obtained online at: http://www.fortuitypress.com/shop or at: http://www.amazon.com.

Fortuity Press
Copyright © 2016 by Fortuity LLC
All rights reserved.

This periodical is indexed in the ATLA Catholic Periodical and Literature Index® (CPLI®),a product of the American Theological Library Association, 300 S. Wacker Dr., Suite 2100, Chicago, IL 60606, USA. Email: atla@atla.com, www: http://www.atla.com.

No part of this volume may be reprinted, reproduced, or utilized in any form by any electronic, mechanical, or other means, now known or hereafter invented, including photocopying and recording, or any form of information storage, retrieval, or transmitting system, without permission in writing from the publisher. For questions regarding such reprints or usage, contact the publisher, Steven Hamilton, MBA, M.Ed., at: fortuitypress@gmail.com.

Printed in the United States of America.
Cover design by Dr. Kimberly Flint-Hamilton, Steve Hamilton
Cover background image entitled *Keys of the Abbey* by Steve Hamilton © 2016
Cover art by Steve Hamilton. Cover photos by Dr. Kathleen Dorsey Bellow, and by permission of The Journal of the BCTS (JBCTS) and Fortuity Press © 2010.
Interior design by Steve Hamilton, Dr. Kimberly Flint-Hamilton

THE JOURNAL
OF THE
BLACK CATHOLIC THEOLOGICAL SYMPOSIUM (BCTS) VOLUME NINE

EDITORS

Dr. Kimberly Flint-Hamilton, Senior Editor
Stetson University

Dr. Cecilia Moore, Editor
University of Dayton

Dr. Diana Hayes, Book Review Editor
Georgetown University, Emerita

THE BLACK CATHOLIC THEOLOGICAL SYMPOSIUM (BCTS)

2016 OFFICERS

Dr. Kathleen Dorsey Bellow, D.Min., Convener
Dr. Maurice Nutt, CSsR, D.Min., Associate Convener
Dr. Shawnee Daniels-Sykes, Secretary
Dr. Timone Davis, Treasurer
Dr. Katrina Sanders, Archivist
Dr. C. Vanessa White, Past Convener

Dedicated to our brother, mentor, and friend,
Dom. Cyprian Davis, O.S.B.

September 9, 1930 - May 18, 2015

*Eternal rest, grant unto him, O Lord
And let perpetual light shine upon him.*

May he rest in peace. Amen.

x

THE JOURNAL OF THE BCTS

Volume Nine   2016

LETTER FROM THE EDITOR
Dr. Kimberly Flint-Hamilton   1
Farewell, Fr. Cyprian

REFLECTION
Dr. Diane Batts Morrow   7
Appreciation for Fr. Cyprian Davis

POEM
Dr. C. Vanessa White   9
"Dom Cyprian Davis - In Gratitude and Praise"

ESSAY
Bryan N. Massingale, STD   11
The Inspiring and Challenging Legacy of
Cyprian Davis, OSB

ARTICLES SECTION 1
Kathleen Dorsey Bellow, D.Min.   23
Securing the Legacy of Black Catholics through
Archival Donations: Dom Cyprian Davis, O.S.B.
(1930-2015), A Case in Point

Dr. Kimberly Flint-Hamilton   39
Theology, A Portrait in Black: Product of Vatican II
and the Civil Rights Movement; Catalyst for
Future Black Catholic Scholarship

POEM
Steve Hamilton   61
"Just Enough"

ARTICLES SECTION 2
Dr. M. Shawn Copeland   63
The Risk of Memory, The Cost of Forgetting

Dr. Joseph S. Flipper   81
Theological Anthropology in the Theology of
Marriage and Family

BOOK REVIEWS
Dale P. Andrews and Robert London Smith Jr., Editors   99
Black Practical Theology
(C. V. White)

Kelly Brown Douglas   101
Stand Your Ground: Black Bodies and the Justice of God
(K. Dorsey Bellow)

Eddie S. Glaude Jr.   105
*Democracy in Black. How Race Still Enslaves the
American Soul*
(J. Nilson)

Paulinus Ikechukwu Odozor, C.S.Sp.   109
*Morality Truly Christian Truly African Foundational,
Methodological, and Theological Considerations*
(A. Mikulich)

Karen Teel   111
Racism and the Image of God.
(S. Aihiokhai)

CHRONOLOGY
BCTS Annual Meetings   113

Farewell, Fr. Cyprian

Dr. Kimberly Flint-Hamilton
Stetson University
DeLand, Florida

Dom. Cyprian Davis, OSB
September 9, 1930 - May 18, 2015

These past two years have been difficult for the BCTS. On May 18th, 2015, we lost our beloved friend, colleague, mentor, and role model, Fr. Cyprian Davis, OSB, at the age of 84. Six years ago, in 2010, Cecilia Moore, Steve Hamilton and I spent two days with Fr. Cyprian and recorded his reflections on his life. Volume IV of the *Journal of the Black Catholic Theological Symposium* features the essay that resulted from that interview.[1]

> *Very few people have what you have – namely, the
> ability to fulfill your dreams.* [2]

Fr. Cyprian lived his life doing the things he most cared about – living as a Benedictine monk, researching and dedicating his work to supporting black Catholics. Raised in the Presbyterian Church, Fr. Cyprian was attracted to the antiquity and ceremony of the Catholic Church from the time he began reading Medieval history as a child. At the age of 12 or 13, he persuaded his parents to allow him to attend a Catholic mass with his uncle. That was when he fell in love. "I was

---

[1] Parts of this letter are drawn from the Cecilia Moore and Kimberly Flint-Hamilton, "Cyprian Davis, O.S.B.: To Walk a Path, To Be Transformed, and To Transform," *The Journal of the Black Catholic Theological Symposium* IV (2010): 29-56.
[2] Moore and Flint-Hamilton 2010, p. 37.

enthralled! I was in heaven!,"³ he recalled during his oral history interview. After a long search for an order that would admit an African American during the Jim Crow era, he settled on the Benedictine monastery at St. Meinrad Archabbey. Fr. Cyprian professed his monastic vows on August 1, 1951, and was ordained to the priesthood on May 3, 1956.

> Parable of the Talents
> To one he gave five talents; to another, two; to a third, one; to each according to his ability. Then he went away. Immediately the one who had received the five talents went at once and traded with them, and made another five. Likewise, the who had the two talents made another two. But the man who received one talent went off and dug a hole in the ground and buried his master's money. (Matthew 24:15-18)

As a young man, Fr. Cyprian studied sacred theology at The Catholic University of America in Washington, and received his licentiate in 1957. In 1964, he earned a license in the historical sciences from the Catholic University of Louvain. The obstacles he faced while working on his PhD dissertation at Louvain included a doctoral committee member who did not believe he was a serious scholar, depression, a sense that he was inadequate for the monumental task of completing the dissertation, the fear that he would let down both his monastic community, and even the thought that, "if I don't make this, I'll have let down the race!"⁴ Fr. Cyprian persevered, however, and in 1977 he completed the doctorate, which focused on the *familia* (mostly the servants) at the Benedictine monastery in Cluny, Saone-et-Loire, France. He developed his talents unwaveringly, in the face of barriers that would have stopped many of us.

> Parable of the Sower
> A sower went out to sow. And as he sowed, some seeds fell along the path, and the birds came and devoured them. Other seeds fell on rocky ground, where they did not have much soil, and immediately they sprang up, since they had no depth of soil, but when the sun rose they were scorched. And since they had no root, they withered away. Other seeds fell among thorns, and the

---

³ Ibid., p. 31.
⁴ Ibid., p. 46.

thorns grew up and choked them. Other seeds fell on good soil and produced grain, some a hundredfold, some sixty, some thirty. (Matthew 13:3-8)

A generous and kind spirit, Fr. Cyprian shared his vast wealth of knowledge, casting much of it on "good soil." In his own words, "Those who are really scholarly are always open and very generous."[5] He taught Church History at St. Meinrad and was a key faculty member at the Institute for Black Catholic Studies in New Orleans. He wrote six books, chief among them, the groundbreaking *History of Black Catholics in the United States* (Crossroad, 1990). In a real and tangible way, Fr. Cyprian founded the discipline of Black Catholic history. He inspired hundreds, even thousands of people, including Andrew Prevot from Boston College whose reflection echoes what so many of us feel:

Fr. Cyprian's book The History of Black Catholics in the United States opened my eyes when I read it the first time roughly ten years ago in a course taught at the University of Notre Dame by Sr. Jamie Phelps. At that time, I understood myself to be a black Catholic but knew almost nothing about my history. I read each page voraciously. I couldn't get enough of the rich details and stories of my community that had been hidden from me for my entire life and were in this text finally being revealed. I never took the opportunity to communicate to Fr. Cyprian how much his book meant to me, but I trust that he knows now how much it has touched so many hearts, including my own. Thank you Fr. Cyprian for taking me on a journey through a history which was so closely tied to the fundamental questions of my life but which I might otherwise have never known!

Andrew L. Prevot, Ph.D.
Assistant Professor
Boston College

Psalm 137:1-4
By the rivers of Babylon, there we sat mourning and weeping, when we remembered Zion. On the poplars of that land we hung up our harps. For there our captors demanded of us songs, our tormentors for a joyful song:

---

[5] Ibid., p. 43.

"Sing us one of the songs of Zion." But how could we sing a song of the Lord in a foreign land?

Fr. Cyprian spent his career working to transform what for African Americans was a "foreign land" into a place we could call home. To advance the cause of social justice, Fr. Cyprian participated in the demonstrations in Selma. The experience was moving for him. In his words, as a result of this event, he says: "I had become black."[6] He was one of the signatories on the manifesto of the NBCCC in 1968, he was a contributor to the 1979 pastoral letter, *Brothers and Sisters to Us*; a contributor to the 1984 pastoral letter on evangelization, *What We Have Seen and Heard*; a charter member of our own organization, The Black Catholic Theological Symposium, and the editor-in-chief of our *Journal*, which he worked hard to establish; charter member of the National Black Catholic Clergy Caucus (NBCCC); archivist for St. Meinrad Archabbey of the NBCCC, and of the Swiss-American Benedictine Congregation. The book he co-edited with Diana Hayes, *Taking Down Our Harps: Black Catholics in the United States* (Orbis 1998), was named for Psalm 137 which laments the loss of home. Diana Hayes comments on the sojourner status of African American Catholics in her introduction to the book:

> Strangers and sojourners no more, African American Catholics will no longer be required, in the words of the psalmist, to "sing the Lord's song in a foreign land" (ps 137, NRSV). Instead, we are taking down our harps and converting that "foreign land" into a homeland, one rich with the woven tapestries of our voices, lifted in praise and song.[7]

Volume IV of *The Journal of the Black Catholic Theological Symposium* is dedicated to Fr. Cyprian. Half the contributions were made to honor Fr. Cyprian's memory. Bryan Massingale's essay, *The Inspiring and Challenging Legacy of Cyprian Davis, OSB*, offers a reflection on Fr. Cyprian's works and their "ground-breaking," "essential," and "indispensable" nature, but most importantly, with the sense of hope by which he lived his life and modeled for others. Kathleen Dorsey Bellow's article, *Securing the Legacy of Black Catholics through Archival Donations: Dom Cyprian Davis, O.S.B. (1930-2015), A*

---

[6] Ibid., p. 43.
[7] Diana Hayes and Cyprian Davis, Taking Down Our Harps: Black Catholics in the United States (Orbis 1998), p. 2.

Case in Point, highlights some of the important points in Fr. Cyprian's life and work, particularly his archival work, and she recommends guidelines to the membership of the BCTS for archival donation. C. Vanessa White offers a poem *"Dom Cyprian Davis - In Gratitude and Praise"* composed in Fr. Cyprian's honor. In my article, *Theology, A Portrait in Black: Product of Vatican II and the Civil Rights Movement; Catalyst for Future Black Catholic Scholarship,* I explore the context in which this seminal volume, to which Fr. Cyprian contributed, emerged and the way that the book and its contributors, inspired a generation of black Catholics, helped move the American Church on a path toward inclusion. M. Shawn Copeland offers a theological reflection on memory, forgetting, forgiveness, and reconciliation in her article, *The Risk of Memory, The Cost of Forgetting.* Joseph Flipper's article, *Theological Anthropology in the Theology of Marriage and Family*, explores the institution of marriage and recommends that familial and marital situations outside of what the Church has considered the norm—often seen as problems illustrative of the breakdown of marriage in contemporary society—may be regarded through a different, anthropological lens which contributes to a new understanding of marriage and family. Steve Hamilton's poem, *"Just Enough"*, captures the current climate of racial divisiveness in our nation and power of love to heal. Finally, we feature five book reviews: *Black Practical Theology*, edited by Dale P. Andrews and Robert London Smith Jr. (reviewed by C. Vanessa White); *Stand Your Ground: Black Bodies and the Justice of God* by Kelly Brown Douglas (reviewed by Kathleen Dorsey Bellow); *Democracy in Black. How Race Still Enslaves the American Soul* by Eddie S. Glaude Jr. (reviewed by Jon Nilson); *Morality Truly Christian Truly African Foundational, Methodological, and Theological Considerations* by Paulinus Ikechukwu Odozor, C.S.Sp. (reviewed by Alex Mikulich); and *Racism and the Image of God* by Karen Teel (reviewed by Simonmary Asese Aihiokhai).

Photo by Kathleen Dorsey Bellow

6

Appreciation for Fr. Cyprian Davis

I first became acquainted with Fr. Cyprian Davis, OSB in 1993 when I read his seminal work, *The History of Black Catholics in the United States*. I was a graduate student at the time in search of a dissertation topic. It seemed to me that Fr. Cyprian had written this book with graduate students particularly in mind, because he indicated areas of black Catholic history that required further research and where promising archival materials existed. I considered his pronouncement, "There is no adequate history of any of the black Catholic sisterhoods [115]," a commission—if not a mandate—to pursue my study of the Oblate Sisters of Providence. I contacted Fr. Cyprian by mail and he graciously suggested possible directions and sources for my research.

I first met Fr. Cyprian in person at the ACHA meeting in New York in 1997. When I revised my dissertation into a book manuscript, he agreed to serve as one of my readers, again offering valuable insights and suggestions. As a member of the Black Catholic Theological Symposium since 2001, I had the pleasure of interacting with Fr. Cyprian during our annual meetings both intellectually and socially. Throughout our association, he impressed me as a masterfully erudite scholar and a generous and supportive human being. Knowing Fr. Cyprian has enriched my faith, my intellect, and my consciousness as an African American Roman Catholic. He will always remain for me the consummate role model of a scholar, mentor, and pioneer in the discipline of history.

Dr. Diane Batts Morrow
Associate Professor of History and
African American Studies
The University of Georgia

8

"Dom Cyprian Davis - In Gratitude and Praise"
A Poem by Dr. C. Vanessa White
Catholic Theological Union

Inspired by his research
Informed as a reader of his books and articles
Transformed as his student
The man, the monk, the historian, the holy man of God
Dom. Cyprian Davis, OSB
A scholar, a man of faith, and a historian beyond measure,
A detective who uncovered hidden resources and treasures that filled a historical and spiritual void within a people
In the beginning . . . Africa
In the beginning . . . there were Black Catholics

THE BOOK/THE CLASSIC TEXT: *The History of Black Catholics in the United States*

African Roots: Kush, Nubians, Ethiopia; Frumentius, Afonso, Anthony of Egypt, Catherine of Alexandria, Benedict the Moor, Afro-Latino – Martin DePorres, St. Monica and St. Augustine,

A Church in Chains,: Esteban, The Enslaved – The Institution of Slavery, Saint Augustine, Florida, Louisiana, Florida, Maryland

Christ's Image in Black, The Builders of the Faith/Women Religious/Shepherds with Black Skins/The Laity: Henriette Delille, Elizabeth Lange, Mother Matilda Beasley, The Healy Brothers: James, Patrick and Alexander, Charles Uncles, Charles Dorsey, Augustus Tolton, Pierre Toussaint, Jean Baptiste DuSable, Harriet, Thompson, Charles Butler, Federation of Colored Catholics, Daniel Rudd, *The American Catholic Tribune*, The Congress of Colored Catholics, Thomas Wyatt Turner, and so many more

Black and Catholic, Coming of Age: Lena Edwards, Mother Theodore Williams, Harold Perry, SVD, National Black Clergy Caucus, National Black Sisters Conference, Black Catholic Seminarians Association, The Black Catholic Theological Symposium, The Institute for Black Catholic Studies, *What We Have Seen and Heard* and *Brothers and Sisters to Us*

We have a testimony to give,
We have a spirituality to share,
We have a history to teach,
To know your history, is to know your greatness.
Thank you Fr. Cyprian.

The Inspiring and Challenging Legacy of Cyprian Davis, OSB[1]

Bryan N. Massingale, STD
Fordham University
Bronx, New York

I have been invited to speak of Fr. Cyprian as a member of the more recent generation of Black Catholic scholars, and to focus on what Cyprian meant to us and the lessons – even challenges – he leaves to the generation that now inherits his mantle.

I had the privilege of knowing Fr. Cyprian in multiple capacities: as a fellow Black Catholic priest and our membership in the National Black Catholic Clergy Caucus; as a faculty colleague at the Institute for Black Catholic Studies at Xavier University (New Orleans); and as a fellow Black Catholic scholar and our membership in the Black Catholic Theological Symposium. Yet these are but only the formal settings of our professional relationships. More importantly and significantly, Cyprian was for me and many others a role model, a mentor, and even a legend. I always approached him with attitudes of awe, reverence, and respect – and deep admiration, appreciation, and affection.

There are few scholars whose works can be called "seminal," "ground-breaking," "essential," and "indispensable." Cyprian's works richly merit these descriptions. But why? Allow me to answer by means of a metaphor.

We are all familiar with the affliction of Alzheimer's Disease, and the tragedy of watching a person being robbed and stripped of his or her memory. A person without a memory is both rudderless and without anchor, lacking connection, direction, and even identity. Catholics of African descent in the United States were, for too long, suffering from a collective Alzheimer's syndrome. We lacked answers to the basic questions of who were we and how came we here. Is our presence in this "white" church an anomaly? A curiosity? A mistake? A delusion? Or worse, one of the worst forms of cultural brainwashing?

---

[1]Portions of this essay have been revised and augmented from an earlier contribution, Bryan N. Massingale, "Cyprian Davis and the Black Catholic Intellectual Vocation," *U.S Catholic Historian* 28 (Winter 2010) 65-82.

The Journal of the Black Catholic Theological Symposium IX (2016): 11-21.

Cyprian's works gave us our memory; they provided us with an anchor and a connection. His landmark study, *The History of Black Catholics in the United States*,[2] tells our collective story, a narrative that is both tragic and inspiring. He relates the stories of a people who kept deep faith with Catholicism despite belonging to a church that too often betrayed their trust. By rooting us in our past of pain and triumph, he provided a compass to guide and inspire us in the present.

It has been said that amnesia is an enemy of justice. Cyprian's long and sometimes lonely hours in research, reflection, and writing were an indispensable contribution to our on-going quest for genuine equality in society and full inclusion in the Catholic Church. By exercising the historian's craft on our behalf, he told the truth or, at least, debunked some of the comforting fictions and convenient omissions that allow injustice to flourish. It is also said that history can be healing, if we have the courage to face its lessons. Cyprian, as our historian, has been a healer par excellence.

Cyprian's Lessons and Challenges for Black Catholic Intellectual Life

What, then, are some of the enduring lessons and challenges that Cyprian leaves to a younger generation as we strive to continue the path he pioneered? I believe that in his person and scholarship, Cyprian is an exemplar of characteristics that constitute the distinctive horizon of African American Catholic intellectual life.

1) Manifest Concern for the Legacy of Slavery for Church and Society. Engaging what M. Shawn Copeland calls the "virulent residue"[3] of slavery is a cognitive, moral, and existential imperative for Black Catholic scholars. This stems from the fact that "black" was a racial identity formed in the modern consciousness during the European era of "discovery" precisely in order to mark those who were not "white" – that is European and Christian – as the nonhuman or subhuman "other" whose bodies could be exploited for commercial purposes. Thus "black" in the modern worldview is inseparable from slavery, colonialism, and injustice. Thus while "black" identity is neither equivalent nor reducible to "enslaved," the enslavement of Black peoples by those of European

---

[2]Cyprian Davis, *The History of Black Catholics in the United States* (New York: Crossroad, 1990).
[3]M. Shawn Copeland, "Theology as Intellectually Vital Inquiry: A Black Theological Interrogation," *CTSA Proceedings* 46 (1991) 51. Copeland elaborates upon the challenges the virulent residue of white racism poses for the entire guild of Catholic theologians regardless of race in her essay, "Racism and the Vocation of the Christian Theologian," *Spiritus* 2 (2002) 15-29.

descent is an inescapable component of intellectual reflection from the U.S. Black Experience.

Cyprian's writings attest to the central importance of slavery for Black Catholic intellectual discourse. He relates that this was the very reason why he initially resisted the study of American history as a professional historian. In an interview, he confesses: "I had no desire to study American history because I was not interested in reading about slavery, and to read about the problems of race and so forth. That was a painful subject and I didn't want to spend my time doing that."[4]

However, he returned from his studies at Louvain a changed man, a transformation occasioned at least in part by the charged racial climate and consciousness of 1960s America. He describes his new awareness: "The sixties changed me like it changed many others. I had gone to Europe as a rather prim and proper young man . . . . I returned as a black man, part of a 'new breed' with a whole new understanding of Church history . . ."[5] Engagement in civil rights activism and sensitivity to the hunger of Black Catholics to know their place in their church led him to the intellectual confrontation with the painful and tragic history he once strove to avoid.

Cyprian's research demonstrates the decisive impact that slavery has upon the history and moral authority of the Church in the United States. Describing a "church in chains," he documents the deep involvement of religious figures and church authority in the practice and intellectual defense of African chattel bondage. Yet he noted that this is not merely a tragedy of the past. Slavery set the tone for the U.S. Catholic community's subsequent and enduring relationships with African Americans, both Catholic and Protestant:

> Slavery has cast a long shadow over the history of the United States. It has led to civil strife, racial violence, and ethnic resentments that still fester. American Catholic history is covered by that same shadow. . . . Not only laypersons but religious and priests availed themselves of slave labor. . . . (T)he Catholic church in the United States found itself incapable of taking any decisive action or of

---

[4]Mark Pattison, "Black Catholic priest-historian retraces his own history," *Catholic News Service*, (February 12, 2007). Available at http://www.catholic.org. Accessed January 7, 2010. See similar comments related in his 2006 Marianist Award Lecture, *To Be Both Black and Catholic* (Dayton: University of Dayton, 2007) 11. Here Cyprian states: "I did not want to study American history; I did not want to be taken up with questions of slavery and the tragedy of race."
[5]Davis, *To Be Both Black and Catholic*, 12.

enunciating clearly thought-out principles regarding slavery. This factor unfortunately prevented the American church from playing any serious role until the middle of the twentieth century in the most tragic debate that this nation had to face.[6]

Cyprian thus established how the experience of slavery sets the parameters of white/black relations that endure even today. One cannot understand contemporary struggles for racial justice without examining how these were forged in the crucible of Black enslavement. The mindset that enabled white supremacy to establish, promote and defend the enslavement of Black bodies – that is, seeing the Black body as inferior, defective, and a deficient specimen of humanity – has enduring manifestations to this very day. Cyprian's personal and intellectual journey shows how Black Catholic intellectual life cannot evade a confrontation with the reality and continuing aftermath of African enslavement in the Americas.

2) Organic Connection to the Faith Community. From the Black Catholic Theological Symposium's founding, Black Catholic scholars have not understood ourselves as "ivory tower" academics encapsulated in confines of abstract research. Rather, as "scholar-activists" we are vital participants both in our church and in the larger Black community.

Cyprian, despite being committed to a monastic vocation, models this organic membership and intellectual service. He states that he returned from his doctoral studies with "a totally different understanding of the role of monasticism in contemporary society." Specifically, he understood that "the monastic scholar must make one's own the quest for truth and the devotion to justice."[7] Never compromising nor apologizing for his monastic identity, he nonetheless was an essential participant in Black Catholic life in the 20th century. He was the major drafter of the U.S. Catholic Bishops' pastoral letter on the sin of racism, *Brothers and Sisters to Us* (1979). He offered major contributions to the African American bishops' pastoral letter on evangelization, *What We Have Seen and Heard* (1984). He was a major contributor to the Black Catholic Clergy Caucus' racism statement on the 500th anniversary of the first enslaved African's presence in the Americas (a.k.a. the "Sankofa" document).[8] He either keynoted or lectured at every National

---

[6]Cyprian Davis, *History of Black Catholics*, 65-66.
[7]Davis, *To Be Both Black and Catholic*, 12, 17.
[8]*The National Black Catholic Clergy Caucus Statement on Racism: A Sankofa Observance of the 500th Anniversary of the First Enslaved African to Enter the*

Black Catholic Congress gathering since its resumption in1987. Spurning repeated overtures from more renowned centers of learning, he remained faithful to his vocation as a seminary professor and a mentor to pastoral minsters serving the Black Catholic faithful.

Cyprian's intellectual project thus shows that an organic connection to the lived experience of one's racial and faith communities is a sine qua non of Black Catholic scholarship. He challenges those who come after him to also understand that an effective solidarity with our stigmatized community of belonging is an essential part of the African American Catholic intellectual vocation.

3) Speaking Truth to and within the Church as a Means toward Justice. I have argued that a constitutive trait of Black intellectual life is a commitment to fuse the life of the mind with the struggle for justice.[9] For U.S. Black Catholic scholars, this entails a commitment to speak uncomfortable yet necessary truths to and within the Church, challenging its propensity to ally itself both subtly and directly with the nation's endemic culture of anti-black racism.

Cyprian powerfully witnesses this willingness to speak difficult truths. He does this most particularly through his ability to unearth the suppressed and tragic memories of institutional complicity in the subjugation and humiliation of persons of African descent. He also challenged what he called "less than through" and thus self-serving treatments of U.S. church history:

> What kind of view of the American Church do we give our students if they do not know that in St. Martinsville, Louisiana, it was taken for granted that a slave had to have his owner's permission to receive communion? What kind of American sacramental theology did we have in this country when it was the regular practice in much of the southern United States for white Catholics to receive communion first and Blacks to receive last? How many who teach pastoral theology know that this venerable custom was maintained until a very recent past? Historically, we like to speak of the American perspective on Church and freedom with John Courtney Murray and his contribution to political theology. Practically, we should examine that perspective from the viewpoint of parishes in Chicago which were in transition from white to

---

Western Hemisphere (1501-2001) (January 15, 2001). Available at http://www.inaword.com/svd/sankofa.pdf. Accessed January 9, 2010.
[9]Bryan N. Massingale, *Racial Justice and the Catholic Church* (Maryknoll, NY: Orbis Books, 2010).

Black, with bitterness and even violence in some neighborhoods. . . . (W)e will find out about pastors standing on the church steps, barring entrance to baptized Blacks. This was also a vision of Catholic America that belongs to the very recent past and that affects us still.[10]

Cyprian's willingness to speak difficult and demanding truths was not without risks and attendant anxiety. He candidly disclosed his "panic" over the adverse consequences that could follow when he signed a prophetic manifesto, written by the inaugural gathering of Black Catholic clergy, which indicted the U.S. Catholic church as a "white racist institution."[11] Yet, he reminds us of the greater danger of silence when confronted with the reality of injustice: "History . . . has taught us that no one can remain silent in periods of great social turmoil and still retain any moral authority. It has also taught that there is no such thing as a political issue without moral consequences."[12] The danger of silence and evasion, he posits, is the betrayal of the Church's mission and integrity: "It is the Church's mission to transform society. It is a Catholic's duty to correct a wrong opinion regarding human rights."[13] Cyprian thus provides for those who come after him a model of courageous truth-telling for the sake of justice.

4) Generosity of Spirit toward Racial Adversaries – even in the Church. One cannot read Cyprian's historical accounts of Black Catholic believers and not be struck by a constant and poignant dialectic: the institution's callousness, neglect, and abandonment vis-a-vis the faithful's obstinate clinging to a faith that gave them sustenance though no welcome. Cyprian relates that Black Catholics had to fight for their faith, but "their fight was often with members of their own household."[14] They were a group that "she [the Church] treated as stepchildren, the last considered and the first to be jettisoned when funds and personnel were scarce."[15] (One sees again how Cyprian was far from being a timid and retiring monk!)

Yet throughout Cyprian's accounts, and particularly in his own person, one finds a generosity and magnanimity of spirit toward racial adversaries. Dictionaries describe "magnanimity" as "greatness of mind

---

[10]Cyprian Davis, "Reclaiming the Spirit: On Teaching Church History: Why Can't They Be More Like Us?" in *Black and Catholic: The Challenge and Gift of Black Folk*, Jamie T. Phelps, ed. (Milwaukee: Marquette University Press, 1997) 46-47.
[11]Davis, *To Be Both Black and Catholic*, 16.
[12]Davis, *History of Black Catholics*, 117.
[13]Davis, "Reclaiming the Spirit: On Teaching Church History," 48.
[14]Davis, *History of Black Catholics*, 259.
[15]Davis, *History of Black Catholics*, 136.

and heart," "a refusal to be petty," "a heart big enough not to hold grudges," "generous in forgiving insult and injury," and "the ability to encounter danger and trouble with tranquility and firmness, while disdaining injustice, meanness, and revenge." Any fair-minded observer appreciates how such characteristics mark Black Catholics not only as a group, but also our intellectual projects. This seems to be rooted in an ability to distinguish between the core essentials of Catholic faith and its flawed institutional manifestations. Stated more colloquially, Black believers survive in the Catholic Church by recognizing that God is bigger than the church, and that the church is bigger than its leaders and wayward members.[16]

We have seen how Cyprian did not shrink from speaking demanding truths to the Church, forthrightly identifying its racist complicity and calling by name those who participated in wrongdoing. All the more, then, that one cannot fail to be moved by how he concluded a reflection upon his life's vocation, as he praised God for the gift of his Catholic faith and professed his love for the Church:

> I shall always be grateful that God called me to serve him in the monastic way of life. . . . And I give thanks to God that I have been able to contribute to the building up of the Catholic Church. Daniel Rudd . . . was an ex-slave who sincerely loved the Church and the African American people. He said that black Catholics were to be the leaven in society. I hope that I have been a part of that.[17]

5) Universalism, Evidencing a Broadly Inclusive Perspective. The noted African American philosopher, Cornel West, summons Black intellectuals to be "race-transcending prophets" who neither ignore the significance of race nor limit themselves to racial activism and investigation.[18] Cyprian's work is animated by such a universal and inclusive perspective. He thus manifests a truly "catholic" outlook, one that stems from his deeply catholic understanding of the church. He related this understanding through using an architectural metaphor to describe his normative vision of the church:

> I like to picture the Church as a very large family living in an ancient, rambling old house with solid foundations, enormous apartments, and a jumble of architectural styles

---

[16]Cyprian relates this realization in his account of his conversion to Catholicism, stating that he "learned that the holiness of the Church does not depend upon the holiness of its members." See *To Be Both Black and Catholic*, 9-10.
[17]Davis, *To Be Black and Catholic*, 17.
[18]Cornel West, *Race Matters* (Boston: Beacon Press, 1993) 46.

that somehow never clash. Enormous cellars, musty libraries, huge fireplaces, grand staircases turning into narrow twisting ladders and sometimes disappearing all together, bricked up windows and doorways barely masking the sound of unseen voices on the other side, meandering corridors, lofty ceilings, narrow cubicles, secret passageways, gorgeous chandeliers and marvelous frescoes partly discolored, all of this together found in this old house. Somehow we all live here, some are here whom we do not see, some we see but we cannot reach, some are lost and we do not know how to reach them. But the old house stands, for it was built on rock.[19]

Cyprian thus summons those of us who share his scholarly vocation to also model this broad universalism and, in the words of West, to "put forward a vision of fundamental social change for *all* who suffer from socially induced misery."[20]

6) Concern for the Ordinary, the Absent and the Invisible. It strikes me that the writings of Black Catholic scholars often reveal modes of analysis that privilege vivid and concrete description over sterile and abstract speculation. This perhaps stems from a commitment to make visible those who have been erased from or rendered voiceless in the dominant accounts of knowledge. We see this in Cyprian's intellectual work as he surfaced the protests of the unlettered that languished in nearly forgotten archives and retrieved the dormant memories of 19th century Black Catholic lay activism. In part, this is a consequence of his academic training, which taught him "to turn to the study of ordinary folk, to be concerned with those in the grass roots, to be interested in the humblest of society . . . the overlooked, the forgotten, the marginal."[21] His identity as a Black man led him to use his skills and sensitivity on behalf of those marginalized by our nation and church. He challenges we who remain to "go and do likewise" (Luke 10:37).

7) Witness of Hope. I have often reflected upon the inscription Cyprian wrote when he signed my copy of his seminal monograph: *"That our history bring knowledge and hope."* Because of the pervasive intransigence of white supremacist anti-blackness in our world, hope is a critical issue for Black people. For the enemies of justice are not only hatred, indifference, ignorance, and fear, but also weariness, cynicism,

---

[19]Davis, "Reclaiming the Spirit: On Teaching Church History," 52.
[20]West, *Race Matters* (Boston: Beacon Press, 1993) 46; emphasis added.
[21]Davis, *To Be Both Black and Catholic*, 11.

resignation, and despair. Cyprian's works are a legacy that testifies to the power of memory to inspire future hope: a hope rooted not only in a community's dogged refusal to acquiesce to the limits imposed by society and church, but also in the God who claimed and stamped Black bodies with an indelible mark of dignity and worth.[22] These, then, are among the signal features of Cyprian's life and intellectual legacy. Without exaggeration, he is an exemplar of a new tradition of Catholic scholarship and intellectual life. This legacy now stands as both an inspiration and a challenge to those who now and in the future will press ahead along the paths that he cleared for us – and perhaps take Black Catholic thought in new directions inspired by his contributions.

I want to conclude on the note of hope that Cyprian wanted to impart through his life and scholarship. Cyprian's historical accounts reveal that, despite how we might feel in the face of the contemporary struggles and challenges that confront Black people in general and Black Catholics in particular, we are not living in the worst of times. There have been eras, even centuries, of graver trials and difficulties for persons of African descent in the U.S. and in the Catholic Church. Yet, Cyprian shows us that we have survived and thrived in the midst of terrible and dreadful circumstances. Even more, in the midst of such trials, Black Catholics have provided the church with models of sanctity, leaders of conviction, and teachers of vision. I have no doubt that when a successor writes a future *History* that chronicles the contributions of this era's Black Catholics, Fr. Cyprian Davis will take his place among those models of sanctity, leaders of conviction, and teachers of vision.

May Fr. Cyprian rest in peace. May the Black Catholic Theological Symposium be worthy bearers of his mantle.

Bryan N. Massingale
Fordham University

A Bearer of Hope: a lesson he gives–despite the evidence to the contrary, these are not the worst of times. There have been other times of grave difficulty for persons of

---

[22]Cf. *"Stamped with the Image of God": African Americans as God's Image in Black*, edited by Cyprian Davis and Jamie Phelps (Maryknoll: Orbis Books, 2003).

African descent in the U.S. and in the Catholic Church. Yet, we have survived and thrived. And have provided the church with models of sanctity, leaders of conviction, and teachers of vision. Without doubt, when a successor writes a *History* that chronicles the Black Catholics of this era, you will be numbered among those models of sanctity, leaders of conviction, and teachers of vision.

Works Cited

Copeland, M. Shawn. "Theology as Intellectually Vital Inquiry: A Black Theological Interrogation," *CTSA Proceedings* 46 (1991) 51.

Copeland, M. Shawn. "Racism and the Vocation of the Christian Theologian," *Spiritus* 2 (2002): 15-29.

Davis, Cyprian. *The History of Black Catholics in the United States.* New York: Crossroad, 1990.

Davis, Cyprian, Marianist Award Lecture, *To Be Both Black and Catholic.* Dayton: University of Dayton, 2007.

Davis, Cyprian. "Reclaiming the Spirit: On Teaching Church History: Why Can't They Be More Like Us?" in *Black and Catholic: The Challenge and Gift of Black Folk*, Jamie T. Phelps, ed. Milwaukee: Marquette University Press, 1997: 46-47.

Davis, Cyprian and Jamie T. Phelps, editors. *"Stamped with the Image of God": African Americans as God's Image in Black.* Maryknoll: Orbis Books, 2003.

Massingale, Bryan M. "Cyprian Davis and the Black Catholic Intellectual Vocation," *U.S Catholic Historian* 28 (Winter 2010) 65-82.

Massingale, Bryan M. *Racial Justice and the Catholic Church.* Maryknoll, NY: Orbis Books, 2010.

National Black Catholic Clergy Caucus Statement on Racism: A Sankofa Observance of the 500th Anniversary of the First Enslaved African to Enter the Western Hemisphere (1501-2001) (January 15, 2001). Available at http://www.inaword.com/svd/sankofa.pdf (accessed January 9, 2010).

West, Cornel. *Race Matters.* Boston: Beacon Press, 1993.

Securing the Legacy of Black Catholics through Archival Donations: Dom Cyprian Davis, O.S.B. (1930-2015), A Case in Point

Kathleen Dorsey Bellow, D.Min.
Institute for Black Catholic Studies
Xavier University New Orleans

> When a man is wise to his own advantage,
> the fruits of his knowledge are seen in his own person;
> When a man is wise to his people's advantage,
> the fruits of his knowledge are enduring.
> (Sirach 37:21-22)

Abstract: Cyprian Davis, O.S.B was a lifelong scholar of church history and a prolific archivist. This article recaps his development as a Catholic historian whose struggle with black consciousness and commitment to serve God's people placed him in a unique position to chronicle the growth of the U.S. Black Catholic church. In late 2014, he made a plan with colleagues to finally organize and dispose of the substantial collection of documents, files, photos, correspondence, and articles related to the history of Black Catholics in the United States that he had accumulated during the course of his career and ministry. Fr. Davis' death, just a few months later, required a drastic change of those plans. His colleagues were left with the task of researching institutional archives, making key decisions, discerning and advocating with his religious community for the disposition of the invaluable paper trail of Fr. Cyprian's life work according to his unwritten plans. As a result of this experience, the author advises Black Catholic scholars to evaluate the historical significance of their personal and professional papers for future researchers, put in writing their intentions to make an archival donation and share their written plans with others.

Keywords: Cyprian Davis, O.S.B., Black Catholic History, and Archival Donations.

Clarence John Davis was born September 9, 1930 in Washington, D.C. to Clarence W. and Evelyn Jackson Davis. Through his great love of history, he encountered the Catholic Church and, as a teen, was initiated into the faith. He attended public schools in the District and graduated from Dunbar High in 1948. By 1949, Clarence John had transitioned from middle-class Negro life in the nation's capital to Benedictine formation at St. Meinrad Seminary in Indiana.[1] Clarence received the name Cyprian when he professed vows as a Benedictine monk in 1951. He was ordained to the priesthood in 1956 and began a long teaching career at St. Meinrad. He returned to D.C. in 1957 as Fr. Cyprian Davis, O.S.B. to study Sacred Theology at the Catholic University of America.

Advanced study in church history led Cyprian to the Catholic University of Louvain in Belgium. There he received the license in historical sciences in 1963 and upon return to the United States in August of that year, found himself in the March on Washington alongside other Benedictine confreres, captivated by Dr. Martin Luther King, Jr.'s "I Have a Dream" speech. He was interested in Black history and participated in one of the 1965 Selma to Montgomery Marches for voting rights; however, Davis did not actively engage in the U.S. Civil Rights Movement. The ugliness of its history and the turbulence of the struggle played out on a daily basis in the news was perhaps too personally complex and spiritually demanding for the young priest.

At St. Meinrad Seminary and School of Theology, Cyprian specialized in church history but became increasingly drawn into the contemporary struggle for racial equality through the inquiries of Black Americans encountered in pastoral settings, retreats and speaking engagements who wondered where the Catholic Church stood on the question of the day. "All those times were in ferment, especially in regard to civil rights, and that's when I began to realize its importance. People began to come and ask me about being black and Catholic: 'What is my place in the church?', he recalled. "That's when I began to realize that this is important. ... That's when I began to do my own research."[2]

In 1968, Cyprian helped found a Catholic fraternity – the National Black Catholic Clergy Caucus (NBCCC) – in whose trusted company and solidarity he would prayerfully deliberate, confer and ultimately challenge the paradoxical position of the Church given the teachings of

---

[1] For information about Fr. Cyprian and his life journey, see Cecilia Moore and Kimberly Flint-Hamilton, "Cyprian Davis, O.S.B: To Walk a Path, To Be Transformed, And To Transform," *The Journal of the Black Catholic Theological Symposium* 4 (2010), 29-56.
[2] "Benedictine Fr. Cyprian Davis, Top Chronicler of Black Catholic History, Dies." *Catholic News Service*, 20 May 2015,
<http://ncronline.org/news/people/benedictine-fr-cyprian-davis-top-chronicler-black-catholic-history-dies> (5/19/16).

Jesus Christ that it preached[3]. Davis resumed his studies with a concentration on the Middle Ages at the Catholic University of Louvain, receiving the doctorate in Historical Sciences in 1977. Through his postdoctoral research, writings, teaching, preaching and presentations, Cyprian grew in knowledge and understanding of church history. In the context of church history and monastic life, he formally established Black Catholic History as a category of academic study and exploration that helps authenticate the full, conscious and active participation of African peoples through the ages in the development of the Church, the universal Body of Christ. [4]

Responding to the needs of the people, Davis moved with a big and generous heart through seemingly disparate worlds. He lived the vocation of a Benedictine monk at St. Meinrad Archabbey and taught in the Seminary and School of Theology. Archival listings of the *Jasper Herald*, an Indiana newspaper (1964 through the 70s), highlight many of Fr. Cyprian's excursions into the local communities of Jasper County and beyond to preside and preach at Masses, speak on monastic life and other spiritual topics, lead retreats, and teach in other seminary programs. He was on the 1980 inaugural faculty of the Institute for Black Catholic Studies (IBCS) at Xavier University of Louisiana in New Orleans and taught there many summers. As his reputation grew, he crisscrossed the United States at the invitation of many faith communities bringing the Good News. Black Catholic parishes, in particular wanted to hear the stories that verified beyond all doubt the long-standing presence of African and African American faithful, religious and clergy in the life of the Catholic Church. Fr. Cyprian also traveled to Africa on several occasions as a visiting professor of church history.

Davis' evangelizing mission, supported by numerous articles and textbooks, inspired a first generation of Black Catholic theologians, historians and pastoral ministers. He assisted the U.S. Bishops in thinking out and writing two key documents: "Brothers and Sisters to Us", the U.S. Catholic Bishops' Pastoral Letter on Racism (1979) and "What We Have Seen and Heard: A Pastoral Letter on Evangelization

---

[3] "A Statement of the Black Catholic Clergy Caucus" in *"Stamped with the Image of God": African Americans as God's Image in Black,* Cyprian Davis, O.S.B. and Jamie Phelps, O.P., eds. *(Maryknoll: Orbis Books, 2003), 111-14.*
[4] The biographical information for this article was drawn from several published obituaries and articles that reported the death of Fr. Cyprian Davis. Volume IV of the *Journal of the Black Catholic Theological Symposium*, in Part One of an Archival Project more completely chronicles the life of Fr. Cyprian Davis, O.S.B. on the occasion of his eightieth birthday.

from the Black Bishops of the United States" promulgated in 1984. His classic and prize-winning text, *The History of Black Catholics in the United States*, published in 1990, was a culmination of his decades of historical research. Cyprian collaborated with Diana Hayes, a professor of Catholic theology at Georgetown University on *Taking Down Our Harps: Black Catholics in the United States,* a collection of theological essays and with Jamie T. Phelps, O.P., a long-time colleague in the movement and systematic theologian, he co-edited *Stamped in the Image of God: African Americans as God's Image in Black.* His *Henriette DeLille, Servant of Slaves, Witness to the Poor*, tells the story of the foundress of the Sisters of the Holy Family of New Orleans.

In addition to Davis' commitment to tell the story of Black Catholics in the context of world affairs and church history, he worked diligently to preserve the legacy. He served as archivist for several groups, including his Archabbey, the Swiss-American Congregation of Benedictine abbeys, as well as the NBCCC and the Black Catholic Theological Symposium (BCTS), of which he was a member and editor-in-chief of its journal.

In 2012, Davis was named St. Meinrad's first professor emeritus, the same year that he retired from teaching at the IBCS. Two years later, Cecilia More and I, BCTS members and IBCS faculty members, visited with Fr. Cyprian at the Archabbey. It became evident that the BCTS should collaborate more closely with Fr. Cyprian to secure his years of archiving on behalf of Black Catholics by helping him prepare the materials in his custody for archival donation at appropriate institutions. This essay will outline the process undertaken to honorably dispose of the African American collections held by Dom Cyprian Davis, including his substantial body of personal papers, that are invaluable to future studies related to Black Catholics and urge others to consider the issues involved in making plans for their own important papers.

The topic of the BCTS archives was raised at the Symposium's 2014 Annual Meeting and the membership requested that the Executive Committee research the options available to provide Fr. Cyprian the assistance required to transfer its years of files to a proper depository[5]. Moore and I were dispatched to meet with the archivist, which we did in December 2014. We found Cyprian in great spirits, working on the

---

[5] In October 2014, the BCTS Executive Committee consisted of Timone Davis, Treasurer; Shawnee Daniels-Sykes, Secretary; Maurice Nutt, CSsR, Associate Convener; Kathleen Dorsey Bellow, Convener and C. Vanessa White, Past Convener.

update of his book, *The History of Black Catholics in the United States* and looking forward to attending a January 2015 historical conference in New York. He reported that since the summer, he was more attentive to his diet and exercising with a trainer. Father introduced us to St. Meinrad seminarians and students from Togo: David N'Djam, O.S.B. and Phillippe Tchalou, O.S.B. One evening after the community's Night Prayer, we all gathered in Fr. Cyprian's office to share Benedictine hospitality and good conversation. Professor Harry Hogan, O.S.B., whose office was next door, joined the company – a break from the labors of the day.

Touring the St. Meinrad archives and the library, Dr. Moore and I discovered the extent of Davis' recordkeeping on behalf of the Benedictines of St. Meinrad, the Swiss-American Congregation of Benedictine abbeys, and the NBCCC, whose files he had been collecting since its inception in 1968. Besides an extensive collection of Clergy Caucus papers, Fr. Cyprian had accumulated a trove of personal Black Catholic historical documents that were stored in a space on the lower floor of the St. Meinrad library. The library director welcomed us as Cyprian's BCTS associates, urging us to provide much needed assistance in organizing and transferring the archived materials as soon as possible.

So, with Fr. Cyprian we devised a general plan for the BCTS files that involved 1) researching potential archive sites; 2) identifying assistants to help catalogue the collection; 3) collaborating with NBCCC leadership as they relocated their documents; and 4) completing the project by Summer 2015. Moore, also a church historian, and Davis discussed at considerable length which Catholic archives would potentially have the interest, space and resources to manage this unique collection. It was decided that a letter would be drafted to each site under consideration to inquire about key issues such as archival requirements, associated costs, copyright transfers and terms of access for future researchers. The list of potential archives identified included: Xavier University of Louisiana (XULA) in New Orleans, Louisiana; University of Notre Dame, South Bend, Indiana; Catholic University of America (CUA) in Washington, D.C.; the Josephite Archives in Baltimore, Maryland; Marquette University, Milwaukee, Wisconsin; and St. Meinrad Archabbey, St. Meinrad, Indiana. The Catholic Theological Union's archives was subsequently added to this list at the request of C. Vanessa White.

In an ensuing conversation, Dr. Moore suggested to Fr. Cyprian that, in addition to the BCTS and NBCCC files, he should consider how he might want to dispose of his personal papers, a collection that would be of great use to current and future scholars who will study the history and experience of Black Catholics in the United States, especially in the second half of the twentieth century. They discussed several interesting options and Davis decided that he would await the results of the archival search to determine how he would proceed.

The plan was launched. Of course, undertaking such an ambitious course of action required substantial institutional support. St. Meinrad pledged a dedicated library workspace, some volunteer summer help and a reasonable time allowance to complete the task of relocating Davis' collections. The BCTS Executive Committee was approached in early 2015 to 1) commit funds for needed supplies and 2) recruit rotating volunteer teams to work onsite under Fr. Cyprian's supervision during the summer of 2015. Fr. Kenneth Taylor, president of the NBCCC, a priest of the Diocese of Indianapolis and an alumnus of St. Meinrad, was advised in February 2015 of the pressing situation regarding the files in Fr. Cyprian's custody. Taylor disclosed that the NBCCC board had been in a three-year conversation about its collection and, in consultation with Fr. Cyprian, were close to choosing a site. Understanding well the scope of the task, Fr. Cyprian had requested NBCCC help to organize and catalogue their files before relocation. Taylor was happy to be included in the summer 2015 plan and promised the cooperation of the Caucus.

Dr. Moore drafted and I dispatched letters on behalf of the BCTS, NBCCC and Fr. Cyprian to the directors of the seven archives identified as potential sites. The gist of the message was: "Would you please advise us of what an archive, such as yours, would require of us should we decide to offer these archives to your institution and what might we expect of your institution in return?" Among the specific questions posed were:

- Under what conditions would you accept these archives?

- Would you prefer that we send the materials to you as they are or would you prefer that we do some preliminary organizing of the documents?

- What rights would the BCTS, the NBCCC, and Fr. Davis and his community have to these collections and their potential uses after they are deposited in your archives?

- Do we need to draw up a contract for the deposit of the archives?

- Is there any cost associated with depositing collections in your archives that we would be expected to cover? If so, what are they?"

Responses from the various archives began arriving in the spring. Father Cyprian was updated on the progress of the search when he attended an April 2015 celebration of the 25th anniversary of the publication of *The History of Black Catholics in the United States* hosted by the Institute for Black Catholic Studies at Xavier University in New Orleans. Dr. Moore delivered a lecture in Father's honor on that occasion. In the following weeks, the three of us - Bellow, Moore and Taylor - finalized travel and lodging plans for the appointed work week in August at St. Meinrad. I mailed a note to confirm the dates; Cecilia visited the Archabbey at Fr. Cyprian's request. A week later on Monday, May 18, 2015, the sad word of Fr. Cyprian Davis' death crisscrossed the country. Many of his colleagues, former students and friends joined the Davis family and the Benedictine community for the funeral services at the monastery. Abbot Justin Duvall, O.S.B. reiterated the invitation for the team, now absent Fr. Cyprian, to follow through with their August plans. He promised whatever material support would be needed to organize the Black Catholic collections in library storage and prepare them for shipping to the designated archives.

In early August, Cecilia Moore wrote to apprise the BCTS Executive board of developments regarding the archives. She reported that all but one of the Catholic archives were very interested in receiving Father Cyprian's collections and that one archive declined due to lack of adequate space to store and care for the files. Another of the interested archives indicated that the BCTS was expected to contribute financially to the maintenance of the collection if entrusted to their care. The other archives were excited at the prospect of receiving Davis' papers and had the resources to collate the large collection. No special organization of the documents was required.

Dr. Moore also described her recent professional experience of the Xavier University Archives and Special Collections when she taught history during the summer 2015 session of the Institute for Black Catholic Studies. She used the services of the archives on a daily basis while teaching and in doing her own research. She spoke of a staff that worked well with students and was very knowledgeable of Black Catholic history. She noted that Xavier University is the only Black and Catholic institution of higher learning in the United States and the BCTS is the parent organization from which the IBCS proceeds. And importantly, she projected that the Xavier archives had the space to house the BCTS materials. Based on her assessment and recommendation, the Executive Board voted to deposit the BCTS archives at Xavier University of Louisiana.

The reality of Fr. Cyprian's absence was heartfelt as the team of Moore, Taylor and Bellow assembled at St. Meinrad Archabbey to undertake the voluminous and important task of organizing his years of recordkeeping on behalf of the Black Catholic community. There were numerous boxes stacked on the floor and shelves of the library storage area in which Father had collected correspondence, articles, photos and research files. Each carton had to be unpacked, its contents examined individually and sorted in one of several different piles of documents. These were rearranged in fresh boxes and labelled for delivery to the next archival destination.

The oldest, most ordered set of files were those belonging to the NBCCC. Among the key finds in the general collection were research files related to Davis' work on the National Conference of Catholic Bishops (NCCB)/United States Conference of Catholic Bishops (USCCB) documents "Brothers and Sisters to Us" and "What We Have Seen and Heard" as well as the *Lead Me, Guide Me Hymnal* produced in 1987 under the auspices of the NBCCC. In addition, there were concept papers and proposals for key institutions such as the Institute for Black Catholic Studies and the NCCB/USCCB Black Catholic Secretariat, established in 1986. These documents reflected Cyprian Davis' unreserved commitment to and involvement in the development of Black Catholic leadership and the evangelizing mission of the Church. He was not only recording the history of God's people in the twentieth century, he was wholeheartedly in the flow of history being made.

The correspondence in the archives included personal family letters and cards, postcards, communications from colleagues, former students, brother clergy and sister religious and general fan club members – young and old. There were a number of thank you notes from young people who had experienced Father Cyprian in a confirmation retreat, First Communion Mass or historical talk. Although there was precious little time to explore in depth, we discovered many historic treasures that renewed memories or revealed new insights into the remarkable life of the Benedictine monk and Black Catholic historian. Fr. Timothy Sweeney, O.S.B., the St. Meinrad archivist and a long-time brother monk of Fr. Cyprian – as graduate students, they often traveled together through Europe – made frequent stops by the library workspace and shared personal recollections of their Paris adventures. As we moved across the St. Meinrad campus during the week for meals and prayer, to relax in the evenings on the guesthouse porch, we were greeted by members of the community. So although Fr. Cyprian was physically absent from the project, his spirit guided the collaboration that was formed to preserve his valuable and significant archives.

After just a couple days of work on the archives, Dr. Moore requested a meeting with the Abbott to suggest that Fr. Cyprian's personal papers be donated by the Benedictine community to the archives of the Catholic University of America in Washington, D.C. During their talks in December 2014, Moore had made the suggestion and Davis seemed intrigued by the idea. After all, Washington, D.C. was his hometown. He had earned a graduate degree from the Catholic University and spent many hours throughout his career conducting research in the CUA archives. Very graciously, in the name of his religious community, the Abbot accepted Cecilia's thoughtful recommendation. With that assurance, we resumed our work, packing up 1) 20+ boxes of Black Catholic History papers and a large, framed Ernie Barnes print of a Black Church service belonging to Cyprian Davis, O.S.B. for donation to The Catholic University of America; 2) a large collection of NBCCC archives - a full thirty-two boxes of documents for transport to Indianapolis with Father Taylor where a select team of Caucus members would process the collection before transferring it to their archives of choice; 3) a set of papers for the archives of the National Black Catholic Sisters housed at Marquette University; 4) a small set of documents for the National Office of Black Catholics (NOBC) forwarded to its archives at St. Thomas University in FL; 5) some IBCS documentation and a modest collection of BCTS files all directed to the XULA Library.

Terms of the Deed of Gift Agreement between the BCTS and the XULA Library, University Archives and Special Collections Division that covers the archival donation are as follows:

1. *Access*: This property shall be open to the research public.

2. *Duplication:* The Xavier Archives may duplicate or reproduce this material for purposes of preservation, security, or dissemination for research purposes. Single copy reproduction may be made available to researchers to be used in the pursuit of scholarship.

3. *Property Rights*: Upon transfer to Xavier Archives, ownership of the above described property is conveyed to Xavier Archives.

4. *Copyrights:* It is the responsibility of Xavier Archives to give proper care to protect copyrights in the property.

5. *Additions*: Additions to this property shall be subject to the terms of this deed of gift.[6]

It took several months for the Benedictine community to close Fr. Cyprian's seminary faculty office and transfer the boxes of papers and other items related to his ministry with the Black Catholic community to the St. Meinrad library storage space. In mid-February 2016, they welcomed Cecilia and me back to the Archabbey to process this set of materials. Here we found the bulk of the BCTS archives, notes and research for the updating of the *History of Black Catholics in the United States*, and his work towards the cause for canonization of Henriette DeLille. Over the course of three days, we sifted through this treasure trove of documents, packing up another 20+ boxes of Fr. Cyprian's collection for shipment to the CUA archives, 2 sizeable boxes of BCTS files and 1 carton of IBCS documentation headed to the XULA archives. Specific collections were returned respectively to the Sisters of the Holy Family, the USCCB Subcommittee on African American Affairs, the

---

[6] Irwin Lachoff, Xavier University of Louisiana Library and Special Collections, Deed of Gift Agreement, August 2015.

NBCCC, care of Fr. Taylor, and to academic advisees of Fr. Cyprian Davis. We were again encouraged in our extraordinary task by Benedictines Fr. Sweeney and Brother David N'Djam who attended Fr. Cyprian in his final days. Their narratives of life in community with Cyprian Davis, O.S.B., Father Taylor's remembrances of him in relationship with the Black Clergy brotherhood, and our own shared memories of him as teacher, colleague and traveling partner gave a sense of humanity and holiness to the rows of sealed and addressed boxes that contained mostly paper, lined up and awaiting shipping by the St. Meinrad Benedictines to various archives across the country. With our task of upacking, processing and transferring this invaluable corpus of work dating back to the late 1960s essentially completed, it occurred to us that the true legacy of a child of God is reflected in the integrity of his/her relationships and the faithfulness with which they go about the work that God has given. Cyprian Davis has lovingly and wisely secured the fruits of his knowledge, his labors, and divine inspiration for generations of scholars to come.

Guidelines for BCTS Scholars for Archival Donation

a. Determine whether you have documents related to your own work or that of the Black Catholic community that can help a scholar of today or the future to produce good historical work on Black Catholics.

b. If the answer is "yes," take some time to review your holdings and determine what you want to donate (correspondence, reports, minutes, research notes, ephemera related to Black Catholics such as posters, bookmarks, calendars, cards, anniversary books, special documents, material culture such as statues, medals, dolls, paintings, awards, citations, and so on).

c. Research possible archives and special collections where you might donate your papers and materials. You might want to consider places that already have significant holdings related to Black Catholics or you might want to donate to your alma mater or to an institution with which you have a significant relationship. If you are a religious or a diocesan clergy member, you may also consider donating to the archives of your community or diocese.

d. Decide if you will begin donating right now or if you wish to donate your papers and materials upon your death. If you wish to make a posthumous donation, it is recommended that you put your wishes in your will and/or trust and that you inform your family and friends of your wishes. You can also make arrangements with the institution to which you wish to donate by signing "Deed of Gift" form. Most archives have those readily available. If you are donating posthumously, we recommend that you provide for the packing and shipping of your donation in your will or trust. For example, you may wish to put aside a fixed dollar amount for shipping and handling, say $500.00, or you may simply say that you wish for the shipping and handling of your donation to come from the proceeds of your estate.

e. You have the right to set the terms of how and when your donation may be used by scholars. For example, you could stipulate that 50 years must pass before your papers are open to scholars.

f. Finally, inform the BCTS of your plans for archival donation. We ask that you do this so that the BCTS will know what your wishes are and may help you with the process should you require assistance. We also want to know so we can direct scholars as to where they may find your papers and materials that may help them to do their work in the future.

Securing the Legacy of Black Catholics through Archival Donations

Works Cited

"A Statement of the Black Catholic Clergy Caucus". In "Stamped with the Image of God": African Americans as God's Image in Black edited by Cyprian Davis, O.S.B. and Jamie Phelps, O.P. Maryknoll: Orbis Books, 2003).

"Benedictine Fr. Cyprian Davis, Top Chronicler of Black Catholic History, Dies". Catholic News Service, 20 May 2015. <http://ncronline.org/news/people/benedictine-fr-cyprian-davis-top-chronicler-black-catholic-history-dies> (5/19/16).

Moore, Cecilia and Kimberly Flint-Hamilton. "Cyprian Davis, O.S.B.: To Walk a Path, To Be Transformed, And To Transform". The Journal of the Black Catholic Theological Symposium vol. 4 (2010): 29-56.

Theology, A Portrait in Black: Product of Vatican II and the Civil Rights Movement; Catalyst for Future Black Catholic Scholarship

Dr. Kimberly Flint-Hamilton
Stetson University
DeLand, Florida

Abstract: This paper explores the context in which the manuscript, Theology, A Portrait in Black, emerged and set the stage for those who were then and have continued to evolve as leaders in the Black Catholic Movement, among them, Dom. Cyprian Davis, O.S.B. Its contributors continued on to become scholars, teachers, and leaders in the U.S. Church. The book, and its contributors, inspired a generation of black Catholics and helped move the American Church on a path toward inclusion. It was both a product of its time and a beacon of hope.

Keywords: Black Catholic, Vatican II, Civil Rights, segregation

The year 2015 marked the 35th anniversary of one of the most influential publications in black Catholic history. *Theology: A Portrait in Black* was the culmination of more than a decade of engagement by black Catholics against racial injustice. Inspired by Vatican II and the Black Power Movement of the 1960s and 1970s, this volume changed the world of black Catholic scholarship. It was a first of its kind – in a tradition of black Catholic publications that includes Daniel Rudd's *American Catholic Tribune*,[1] Thomas Wyatt Turner's *The Chronicle*,[2] and the *Cardinal's Notebook* of Victor and Constance Daniels,[3] *Theology: A Portrait A Portrait in Black* was the first publication by black Catholic scholars, about black Catholics, and concerned with the role of blacks in the Church. This small green volume transformed the way black Catholics thought about themselves in the Church, and, even more importantly, inspired the next two generations of black Catholic scholars.

---

[1] Joseph Lackner, "Dan A. Rudd, Editor of the American Catholic Tribune, From Bardstown to Cincinnati," *Catholic Historical Review* 80, No. 2 (1994): 258-281.
[2] Albert Raboteau, "Relating Race and Religion, Four Historical Models," in *Uncommon Faithfulness: The Black Catholic Experience*, ed. M. Shawn Copeland (Maryknoll, NY: Orbis Books, 2009), 9-25.
[3] Cecilia Moore, "Victor and Constance Daniel and Emancipatory Education at the Cardinal Gibbons Institute," *Journal of Catholic Education* 4[3] (2001): 396-404.

This article explores the factors which contributed to the production of the collection, *Theology: A Portrait in Black*, and the profound influence of this volume on black Catholic scholarship in the generations since its publication.

Theology: A Portrait in Black emerged from the chaos of a world in transition. The atomic bomb had only recently destroyed two cities effectively ending World War II; radio had given way to television as the primary news and entertainment medium; new medicines were being developed, including penicillin and oral contraception; the space race was changing the way we thought about our place in our world and in the universe; while civil strife and the threat of world war raged on. Civil rights struggles were coming to a head all over the world. In the words of Charles Dickens, for many, "It was the best of times; it was the worst of times."[4]

The Catholic Church was experiencing change too. In October 1958, a new pope was elected. Angelo Giuseppe Roncalli became Pope John XXIII (now Saint John XXIII). In January 1959, within months of his election as pontiff, Pope John XXIII (now "Saint" Pope John) announced the convening of the Second Vatican Council. In many ways John XXIII was an unconventional pope. He visited children with polio, prisoners, and the juvenile inmates of a reformatory in Rome. He developed the habit of walking the streets of Rome at night, which earned him the nickname, "Johnny Walker."[5] Having come from modest beginnings – his parents were sharecroppers and John was the eldest son of thirteen children – it should have come as no surprise that John believed that the Church of the 1950s was in need of self-evaluation.

Catholics were changing along with the rest of the world. The way they interacted with one another was changing. Inevitably, relationships between blacks and whites in the U.S. were changing too.

> The signs of the times in the mid-20th century pointed to an astounding cultural revolution that threatened to turn the world community on its axis. ... To varying degrees, institutions, communities and families found everyday life turned upside down and inside out. The clash between

---

[4] Charles Dickens, *A Tale of Two Cities* (New York: Dover Thrift Editions, 1999).
[5] David Kerr, "Pilgrims Crowd Bl. John XXIII's Grave On Day He Died," *Catholic News Agency*, June 3, 2011, From Catholic News Agency web site, http://www.catholicnewsagency.com (accessed October 24, 2014). See also, "Look Ahead, Pontiff Advises Young Inmates," *St. Petersburg Times, Associated Press*, November 12, 1962, accessed January 2, 2014.

cultural and counter-cultural ideas and values raised new questions about life with no easy answers. The people of God had become a sign of the times.[6]

The time had come for the Church to think critically about the way the Magisterium interacted with the faithful and to start contemplating difference, as indicated in John XXIII's opening speech, in which he stated, "[E]verything, even human difference, leads to the greater good of the Church."[7] The faithful were urged to contemplate the stars in this address, which later became known as "the speech to the moon."[8]

Vatican II would last from 1962 until 1965. Pope John opened the Council, but would succumb to stomach cancer in 1963, so Pope Paul VI would ultimately be responsible for promulgating the Council documents. For the most part, the laity would interpret the purpose of the Council as extending a hand of welcome to Christians outside of the Catholic faith, as indicated in this excerpt from the New York Times: "The convocation of the ecumenical council ... is intended also as an invitation to the separated communities in quest of unity."[9] This theme of welcome is touched upon in several of the Council documents. But Vatican II did much more than that. Vatican II changed the way Catholics viewed their place in the world and with the "other." Among the documents from Vatican II was *Lumen Gentium* (Light of the Nations), promulgated in November 1964, in which the following two statements appear:

- There is, therefore, in Christ and in the Church no inequality on the basis of race or nationality, social condition or sex, because "there is neither Jew nor Greek; there is neither bond nor free: there is neither male nor female. For you are all 'one' in Christ Jesus;
- Thus in their diversity all bear witness to the wonderful unity in the Body of Christ. This very diversity of graces, ministries and works gathers the children of God into one,

---

[6] Kathleen Dorsey Bellow, "The Black Community and the Call for Vatican Council II (1962-1965)," *The Journal of the Black Catholic Theological Symposium* VIII (2014): 21-53, quote from page 24.
[7] Pope John XXIII, "Opening Speech for Council of Vatican II," October 11, 1962, The Second Vatican Ecumenical Council , Vatican II, Papal Encyclicals Online, accessed October 20, 2014, http://www.papalencyclicals.net/vatican2.htm .
[8] "John XXIII: The Speech to the Moon Above ... ", News.VA, Official Vatican Network, accessed December 14, 2013, http://www.news.va/en/news/john-xxiii-the-speech-to-the-moon-above.
[9] *The New York Times*, January 26, 1959, 3.

because all these things are the work of one and the same Spirit.[10]

These words, and these concepts, would have been very powerful to African Americans in the 1960s. As the '60s raged on in the United States, with the assassinations of President Kennedy, Martin Luther King Jr., Malcolm X, Robert Kennedy, and many others, America endured the turmoil born of centuries-long oppression. African American Catholics, who had long been suffering the sting of inequality, began to find their voices. Inspired by Vatican II, the Black Power movement, and the fight for Civil Rights, they began to ask the critical question – why? Why did the American Catholic Church seem so oblivious to the suffering of black Catholics?

The assassination of Martin Luther King, Jr. in 1968 and the riots that sparked and blazed in the aftermath – including Chicago Mayor Daley's "shoot to kill … shoot to maim" order[11] – prompted Illinois priest Herman Porter to urge all black priests to gather a day in advance of the meeting of the Catholic Clergy Conference on the Interracial Apostolate at the Sheridan-Cadillac hotel in Detroit. The priests who responded formed a caucus. Black priests had never before come together as a body in the Church's history. That act changed the landscape of the Church. These black priests demanded that attention be paid to the plight of African Americans. Historian Cyprian Davis, O.S.B., who participated at that 1968 meeting, reflected on that historic gathering:

> The meeting, which began as a planning strategy to face the situation at that time quickly became a concerted effort to share their experiences and their feelings as black men in that institution that was then seen to be a very white organization. They spoke of their disappointments, their hurt, their bitterness. Not all had had the same experience. Not all were of the same mind, but enough were so that a unity was formed and the

---

[10] Dogmatic Constitution of the Church, *Lumen Gentium*, Solemnly Promulgated by His Holiness Pope Paul VI on November 21, 1964. From the Vatican Archives web site, accessed December 30, 2013,
http://www.vatican.va/archive/hist_councils/ii_vatican_council/index.htm.
[11] James Coates, "Riots Follow Killing of Martin Luther King, Jr.," *Chicago Tribune*, December 19, 2007, accessed October 10, 2014.

decision emerged to challenge the American bishops and to publish a manifesto.[12]

These black priests became the National Black Catholic Clergy Caucus (NBCCC). At the conclusion of that historic gathering, they issued a manifesto which opened with this statement: "The Catholic Church in the United States is primarily a white racist institution, has addressed itself primarily to white society and is definitely part of that society."[13]

This was a courageous statement for a group of priests who would have had to answer to their respective bishops, abbots, and provincials. Davis elaborated on his feelings at that charged meeting. Standing in line to sign the document but still uncertain, he recalled:

> How can the Spouse of Christ be a white racist institution? ... What was flashing in my mind was, this is just like the French Revolution! ... I'm thinking to myself as we were standing in line, 'what will my Abbot say?' But then it came to me. If my Abbot says anything, I'm going to say, 'you must understand that the Catholic Church in its history *was* corrupt, was even moribund! ... And this was one of those times!'[14]

The manifesto continued on to describe the condition of blacks in the Church and to make recommendations regarding the recruitment and use of black priests and deacons, and training for white priests serving predominantly black parishes. It also called for the creation of a department that would assist blacks in their struggle for liberation.[15]

Later that same year, black sisters gathered in Pittsburgh, PA and formed the National Black Sisters Conference. And in 1969, the sisters drew up a position paper in which they stated their goal to work for the liberation of blacks. Shortly thereafter, the National Office for Black Catholics (NOBC) was created in 1970, with Joseph Davis, S.M. as its director.[16]

---

[12] Cyprian Davis, OSB, "To Be Both Black and Catholic," *Marianist Award Lecture 2006* (The University of Dayton, 2007), 15.
[13] Cyprian Davis, O.S.B. and Jamie Phelps, O.P., *Stamped in the Image of God, African Americans as God's Image in Black* (Maryknoll, NY: Orbis Books) 111.
[14] Moore and Flint-Hamilton, "Cyprian Davis, O.S.B.: To Walk a Path, To Be Transformed, and To Transform," *The Journal of the Black Catholic Theological Symposium*, vol. IV (2010): 29-56, esp. p. 45 (emphasis in original).
[15] Davis and Phelps, *Stamped in the Image*, 111-114.
[16] Davis and Phelps, *Stamped in the Image*, 118-119.

At the center of this swirl of activity, which has been called the Black Catholic Movement, was Thaddeus Posey O.F.M. Cap. Posey was a Capuchin Franciscan friar from Washington, D.C. He and his family were active in civil rights struggles in Washington, DC. A seminarian in 1968, Posey was present at that groundbreaking first meeting of the NBCCC. He was appointed secretary of the organization and held this office for over a decade. Posey was ordained in 1971. Like most black priests, he was assigned to predominantly white parishes. While stationed at a parish in Denver, he made this statement to the *Denver Post*:

> It seems anyone interested in social justice is branded a supermilitant nowadays. They're considered just another radical. Maybe people are tired, or maybe they're not aware of the situation. Some think that we've already been through the civil rights struggle and it's all over. But it's not. We have an obligation to continue the struggle for Chicanos, Indians and blacks.[17]

In the *Denver Post* interview, Posey stated that he felt obligated to fight for justice, particularly since the Church had not been attuned to the needs of minorities. Three years later, in 1976, realizing that the Church had not changed nearly enough since that fateful 1968 summer, it occurred to him that, even though there had been black Catholic lay congresses at the end of the 19th century,[18] there had never before been a meeting of Black Catholic scholars and theologians, the black intellectual leaders of the Catholic faith. He set out to make arrangements for such a meeting at the Oblate Sisters of Providence Motherhouse in Baltimore Maryland. With three cousins who were Oblates,[19] the Baltimore motherhouse was both accessible and convenient. After nearly two years of preparation, on October 12, 1978, the dream became a reality. Thirty-three Black Catholic scholars and theologians convened at the Oblate Motherhouse in Baltimore. The meetings took place over a four-day period. At the adjournment on October 15, Posey announced plans to publish the papers that had been delivered and discussed so intensely into a volume, entitled *Theology: A Portrait in Black*. The NBCCC held the copyright and the Capuchin Press in Pittsburgh published it. He envisioned this volume as the first in a series, as indicated from the words "Number One" printed at the bottom

---

[17] Virginia Culver, "People Watch Black Priest," *The Denver Post*, December 21, 1973.
[18] Albert Raboteau, "Relating Race and Religion," 15-16.
[19] Personal communication, September 11, 2011.

of the front cover. A second meeting was convened shortly thereafter, and papers were collected from that meeting but were never published. The book, therefore, became a stand-alone volume, and its contents show the status and form of inquiry into black Catholic consciousness at the end of the 1970s.

Theology: A Portrait in Black bears the stamp of the dialogues, struggles and conflict of the previous decades. Several of the papers were clearly influenced by the many voices of social activism of the 1960s and 1970s. Some papers were emotional, even angry at the blatant racism of so many parishes and communities. Others were more reflective, hopeful for a better world that would be inclusive of the diversity of voices of the Church. Still others were more dispassionate, aiming to evaluate the condition of the American Church through a lens of quiet intellectualism.

In the introduction to the volume, Joseph Nearon, S.S.S. set the tone by positing two goals for black theology. Citing a paper that he had delivered three years earlier at the 1975 CTSA conference,[20] he wrote:

> Black Theology has a two-fold task. First, it may seek to give *a black articulation* of the Christian faith. Secondly, it may strive to give a *Christian interpretation* of the black experience. Obviously these two approaches are closely related. Yet they are not identical and the correct interpretation of any given black theologian must begin by ascertaining which of these two approaches he is taking.

Nearon raised the following questions, which formed the scaffolding along which the remaining twelve papers built their theses: (1) Can one be a Christian if one is black?; and (2) Can one strive for black identity and black power if one is to be a faithful Christian?

The volume was divided into six sections: (1) Black Values; (2) Black Self-Concept; (3) Concept of Celebration; (4) Spirituality; (5) Pastoral Theology; and (6) Catechetics. Each section contained two papers that outlined either a gap in the Church with regard to the spiritual needs of black Catholics, or articulated the way that the black Catholic experience enhanced the teachings of Mother Church.

---

[20] Joseph Nearon, S.S.S., "A Challenge to Theology: The Situation of American Blacks," *Proceedings of the Catholic Theological Society of America* 30 (1975): 177-202, esp. page 183; Joseph Nearon, "Introduction," *Theology, A Portrait in Black*, (Pittsburgh, PA: Capuchin Press, 1980), 5-6, quote from page 5 (emphasis added).

In the section on Black Values, Edward Braxton[21] raised questions about the meaning of black culture. Are there common threads in the black Catholic experience? What constitutes "blackness"? These are difficult questions to answer, since there are black people in nearly early every walk of life.

> The Black Catholic community, for example, is not one world. It is many worlds - the wealthy, the poor; the educated, the less educated; the simple, the sophisticated; the activist, the indifferent; the pious and the doubtful. Conflicts develop in a supposedly homogeneous group because of different horizons of the known, the *known-unknown* [i.e., the things you realize you don't understand], and the *unknown-unknown* [i.e., the things you don't realize you don't understand].[22]

Later in his essay, Braxton reflected on the need and potential for a black Catholic theology:

> Aesthetically, liturgically, and theologically, there could emerge reflections, expressions, and styles of the Black Catholic experience in a hybrid, in the profoundest sense of that term. Such a penetration and reinterpretation of the Black experience could well produce classic expressions that will penetrate the particularity experience in such a way that it illuminates the universal with a telling urgency and enriches the larger Church community with a much needed vitality. While this is a very real possibility, it can be lost by lack of diligence, lack of consistency, lack of collaboration, and lack of sensitivity to the complexities that are involved. In the fact of the present ferment in theology in general, there can be little doubt that the systematic formulation of an authentic Black Theology, for example, will be a slow process, with false starts and misguided condemnations. But the results may well be worth it. [23]

---

[21] Now Bishop of Belleville, Illinois.
[22] Edward Braxton, "Religion, Values, Ethnicity, and the Black Experience," *Theology: A Portrait in Black*, (Pittsburgh, PA: Capuchin Press, 1980), 15-30, quote from p. 24. (emphasis added).
[23] Braxton, "Religion, Values," 30.

In his concluding remarks on black values, Braxton remarked that we all are "living human documents" with our own distinctive histories and interpretations, all of which are of vital importance to the Church. Black Catholics must be prepared to face conflict arising from different interpretations based on differing points of view, yet remain attentive to their critical role in the "shape of the Church to come."[24]

The essay of Jamie Phelps, O.P. on Black Self Concept drew on social science research and the documents of Vatican II. She began by discussing studies of the damage done to the self-image of children who grow up in a society permeated by racism, and points out that a Church that embraces the Vatican II messages of inclusion would support the growth and development of black Catholics and therefore be strengthened.

Phelps' essay calls to mind the experiments of psychologists Kenneth and Mamie Clark who studied the self-concept of black children by giving them two dolls that were identical in every way except their skin color. One doll was white while the other was black. The children were asked to comment on which doll they felt was prettier, nicer, smarter, and the like. The Clark experiments were meant to determine whether there was a link between educational segregation of black and white children and the self-concept of blacks. They concluded that segregation is one of the primary factors eroding the self-image of black children, so much so that the majority of children tested considered the white dolls more attractive, more "good", nicer, and were preferred as playmates, while the black dolls were uglier, "bad", and thought to be less friendly. The Clarks' study was used as evidence in Brown vs. the Board of Education decision of 1954, arguably one of the most significant, if not the most significant, Supreme Court decisions in the twentieth century.[25]

> [A]s minority group children learn the inferior status to which they are assigned – as they observe the fact that they are almost always segregated and kept apart from others who are treated with more respect by the society as a whole – they often react with feelings of inferiority and a sense of personal humiliation. Many of them

---

[24] Braxton, "Religion, Values," 30.
[25] V.P. Franklin, "Introduction: Brown v. Board of Education: Fifty Years of Educational Change in the United States," *The Journal of African American History* 90, *No. 1/2, Brown v. Board of Education: Fifty Years of Educational Change in the United States, 1954-2004*, (2005): 1-8, quote from page 4.

become confused about their own personal worth. ... The report indicates that minority group children of all social and economic classes often react with a generally defeatist attitude and a lowering of personal ambitions.[26]

In fact, the results of the Clark study were confirmed by personal testimony, e.g., by Ethel Belton, who had tried to find transportation to and from school for her tenth-grade daughter Louise. During the trial that followed in 1951, she replied to a question about the effects of school segregation on her daughter:

> To my understanding and my knowledge we are all born Americans, and when the State sets up separate schools for certain people of a separate color, then I and others are made to feel ashamed and embarrassed, because such separations humiliate us and make us feel that we are not as good Americans as other Americans, and I don't want my child growing up feeling that she is not as good an American as any other American, so much that the school she goes to, she has to be separated or set apart to attend a separate, special school.[27]

This sentiment is consistent with that of Carter G. Woodson, expressed in 1933:

> The same educational process which inspires and stimulates the oppressor with the thought that he is everything and has accomplished everything worthwhile, depresses and crushes at the same time the spark of genius in the Negro by making him feel that his race does not amount to much and never will measure up to the standards of other peoples. ... The difficulty is that the

---

[26] Kenneth B. Clark, Isidor Chein, and Stuart W. Cook, "The Effects of Segregation and the Consequences of Desegregation, A {September 1952) Social Science Statement in the Brown v. Board of Education of Topeka Supreme Court Case," reprinted in *American Psychologist* 59 (September 2004): 495-501, quote from pp. 495-496.

[27] Brett Gadsden, "'He Said He Wouldn't Help Me Get a Jim Crow Bus': The Shifting Terms of the Challenge to Segregated Public Education, 1950-1954", *The Journal of African American History, vol. 90, No. 1/2, Brown v. Board of Education: Fifty Years of Educational Change in the United States, 1954-2004* (2005): 9-28, quote from page 14.

"educated Negro" is compelled to live and move among his own people whom he has been taught to despise.[28]

Yet, in her essay, Phelps elaborated on the Clarks' findings by pointing out the number of black children who managed to form positive self-concepts because of positive black role models.

> Children nurtured in the milieu of positive self-affirmation within his/her Black family and Black community, can attain a positive self-concept. Such children attain a sense of competence because they begin to view the Black world around themselves as a realm within which they can cope. Their perception is strengthened when they are permitted to have some power over their destiny. Successful experiences in coping well in their nurturing community assures one of the ability to satisfactorily meet the new challenges which arise and result in achievement in the spheres of both the Black and White worlds.[29]

Phelps developed her thesis on self-concept through the lens of two papal encyclicals. In Pope John XXIII's *Pacem in Terris*, racial discrimination is challenged: "The conviction that all men [women] are equal by reason of their natural dignity, has been generally accepted. Hence racial discrimination can no longer be justified"[30] And in Pope Paul VI's *Populorum Progresso*, racism is identified as a divisive agent: "Racism is still an obstacle to collaboration among disadvantaged nations and causes a division and hatred within countries whenever individuals and families see the inviolable rights of the human person held in scorn, as they themselves are unjustly subjected to a regime of discrimination because of their skin color."[31] Finally, Phelps cited the Vatican II decree, *Ad Gentes:*

> For the Church is more firmly rooted in a people when the different communities of the faithful have members of salvation who are drawn from their own members –

---

[28] Carter G. Woodson, *The Mis-Education of the Negro*, (New York: Dover edition, 2005 [1933]), ix-x.
[29] Jamie Phelps, O.P., "Black Self-Concept," *Theology: A Portrait in Black*, (Pittsburgh, PA: Capuchin Press, 1980),52-65, quote from page 55.
[30] Pope John XXIII. *Pacem in Terris*, as quoted in *Social Justice: The Catholic Position*, ed. Vincent P. Mainelli (Washington, D.C.: Consortium Press, 1975), #309.
[31] Pope Paul VI, *Populorum Progresso*, as quoted in *Social Justice: The Catholic Position*, ed. Vincent P. Mainelli (Washington, D.C.: Consortium Press, 1967), #866, 867, 868.

bishops, priests, deacons, serving their own brothers (sisters) so that these young churches gradually acquire a diocesan structure of their own clergy.[32]

Phelps made the point that, in order to bring Blacks into authentic communion with the Church, local churches need to foster the development of a positive black self-concept. This would allow blacks, "to discover for themselves in full fidelity to their own proper genius the means for their spiritual, physical, and psychological progress," but it would require significant re-structuring of the American Church which, in her words, "tends to identify with the racist aspects of this nation's institutions."[33]

In the section on Celebration, liturgist and composer Clarence Rivers wrote about double standards, the tragedy of forced assimilation, and the oppressive nature of the Jim Crow South where he was born. Blackness is something that should be celebrated, he maintained. Black churches have the power to foster a positive self-concept. To paint the portrait of a black theology, one needs the right tools, and for Rivers, liturgy was the answer. He wrote:

> Up until now all that has been achieved in bringing together black culture and Catholic worship in the U.S. has been achieved by individuals and individual parishes. There has been no ongoing official Church program except the attempts of NOBC's [National Office of Black Catholics] department of culture and worship, to promote the integration of black culture and Catholic worship. In fact most of what has been done has been done in spite of the official Church rather than because of it.[34]

Rivers believed that there was need for an authentic black expression of worship within the Church. And this was a change that only blacks had the capacity to effect. Consistent with the theme of *Lumen Gentium,* Rivers believed that black Catholics should be able to partake of full membership in the Church by contributing their own distinctive graces and ministries. Rivers' efforts bore fruit. He inspired

---

[32] Decree *Ad Gentes* on the Mission Activity of the Church, From the Vatican Archives web site, accessed January 2, 2014,
http://www.vatican.va/archive/hist_councils/ii_vatican_council/index.htm.
[33] Phelps, "Black Self Concept," 60.
[34] Clarence Rivers, ""Thank God We Ain't What We Was: The State of the Liturgy in the Black Catholic Community," *Theology: A Portrait in Black*, (Pittsburgh, PA: Capuchin Press, 1980), 66-74, quote from page 72.

the hymnal, *Lead Me, Guide Me,* which the NBCCC published and dedicated to him in 1987.

The strong influence of the Black Power Movement, Black Liberation Theology, the Nation of Islam, and the Pan-African values system of Ron Maulana Karenga are evident in the paper by Al McKnight, C.S.Sp., entitled "A Black Christian Perspective of Spirituality." McKnight opened with an emotional commentary on the devaluation of black life in the United States and the frightening degree to which blacks are affected by drugs, violence, depression, and mental illness. Citing the work of Albert Cleage,[35] he denounced the "declaration of black inferiority" and the way the term "nigger" had been ascribed to black men.

> The task of Black Spirituality must be the task of transforming niggers into persons. Elijah Muhammad of the Nation of Islam understood this and succeeded in developing self-respecting human beings out of niggers despite his erroneous doctrine. Why have we, who proclaim to have the true doctrine, failed so miserably in the Black community? I think we failed to develop a truly Black practice of the Christian Faith because we have failed to develop our Black authenticity, our Black goodness, our Black truth.[36]

McKnight acknowledged the debt he owed to the Black Power Movement in the South. He urged careful planning and discipline to correct the deep problems that plague black society. McKnight advocated:

> Finally, this will be a plan to which we can emotionally commit our lives. We need a one-year, five-year and fifty-year plan for human development. We will be realistic and rational and "wholistic" by working and struggling under a plan. It is not enough for us to say that we are committed to our own spiritual development if we do not have the capability (the ability and the will) to effectively and

---

[35] Albert Cleage, *Black Christian Nationalism: New Directions for the Black Church* (New York: W. Morrow, 1972), xxv –xxvi.
[36] A. M. McKnight, "A Black Christian Perspective on Spirituality," *Theology: A Portrait in Black*, (Pittsburgh, PA: Capuchin Press, 1980), 103-112, quote from p. 104.

efficiently struggle for our own development. In order to be capable, we must be strong African people.[37]

The paper of Elbert Harris, S.S.J. who, after submitting his paper, passed away days before the symposium, and to whom *Theology: A Portrait in Black* is dedicated, cautioned against allowing this important meeting to degenerate into a myopic airing of grievances without forming concrete corrective strategies that will benefit not just African Americans, but the whole Church.

> We have confidence that we may offer a significant contribution to the advancement and enhancement of the integrity of the entire Church. Our desire is to make the Mystical Body of Christ as perfect in reality as it is in theory. We are not meeting solely for our own personal, individual, or even collective advancement as Black Catholics. Increased self-esteem may result as an extrinsically logical consequence and by-product of our conference. Yet it will be only a more insightful recognition of what we really are, secure and worthy of God's love.[38]

Harris continued with a long series of questions designed to evaluate the degree to which Church was or was not working to eliminate racism in individual parishes and in the community, as well as the level of support for the black Apostolate. He concluded by writing: "Our focus on the Black Community and Black institutions is not an end in itself. The end is neither 'separation,' as we know it, nor 'integration,' as we know it, but congregation, which the unifying Spirit of God will show is."[39]

In the section on Spirituality, Cyprian Davis set out to take the canonical model of spirituality which was highly abstract, and make it more tangible. Davis laid out four Black models of spirituality in the Catholic tradition, and added a fifth, the life of Sojourner Truth. The narratives of St. Moses the Black, St. Benedict the Black, and Sojourner Truth have in common the thread of humility. St. Moses the Black lived in the late 4th or early 5th century. According to the sources, Moses had been somewhat of a brigand. He had been a slave to a government

---

[37] McKnight, "A Black Christian Perspective," 111-112.
[38] Elbert Harris, S.S.J., "Issues Concerning the Development of the Catholic Church in the Black Community," *Theology: A Portrait in Black*, (Pittsburgh, PA: Capuchin Press, 1980), 126-131, quote from p. 126.
[39] Harris, "Issues Concerning", 131.

official in Egypt, had been accused of theft and murder, and as a result, had been dismissed from servitude – an unusual way of dealing with a recalcitrant slave. Davis interpreted this as a sign of just how fearful Moses' owner had been of him – he was, according to sources, a large, imposing man who inspired real fear. Moses then went into the desert, at the time, the home of society's rejects, including tax-evaders, bandits, and the like. But Moses converted to Christianity and became a monk. He gained a reputation for his humility rather than his fearsomeness. Davis related several stories about St. Moses that are found among the 16th century Apophthegmata, or the Sayings of the Fathers. The narrative about Moses is especially informative:

> Another day when a council was being held in Scete, the Fathers treated Moses with contempt in order to test him, saying, 'Why does this black man come among us?' When [Moses] heard this he kept silence. When the council was dismissed, they said to him, 'Abba, did that not grieve you at all?' He said to them, 'I was grieved, but I kept silent.'
> ... It was said of Abba Moses that when he was ordained and the ephod was placed upon him the archbishop said to him, 'See Abba Moses, now you are entirely white.' The old man said to him, 'It is true of the outside, lord and father, but what about Him who sees the inside?'[40]

Davis pointed out that the stories about St. Moses the Black emphasize his humility. And Moses' humility rests heavily on the fact that his skin is black.

The second narrative is that of St. Benedict the Black. Benedict lived in 16th century Sicily. He was the son of two African slaves, and was free when he was 18. His humility in the face of taunts about his blackness and his slave origins attracted the attention of Jerome Lanza, the leader of a group of hermits. Benedict joined the hermits, and upon Lanza's death, became leader of the group. When Pope Pius IV invited the hermits to join the established orders, Benedict became a lay brother of the Friars Minor at Palermo. He eventually became superior of his group and novice master – a highly unusual position for a former slave who had never been ordained a priest and who was probably illiterate. Like Moses the Black, Davis noted that the stories about Benedict emphasize his humility.

---

[40] Cyprian Davis, "Spirituality," *Theology: A Portrait in Black*, (Pittsburgh, PA: Capuchin Press, 1980), 91-102, quote from p. 93.

Davis demonstrated how Sojourner Truth's narrative exemplified key aspects of the spiritual tradition, even though she was not Catholic. Truth was born into slavery but emancipated in 1827 when slavery was abolished in New York. Sixteen years later, at the age of 46, she felt called to a spiritual mission. It was then that she changed her given name (Isabelle) to one more fitting of a "sojourner of the truth." Sojourner Truth developed a habit of praying everywhere, all the time. She became a contemplative and practiced unceasing prayer. Her name change, her life as a wandering pilgrim, and her contemplative nature, in Davis' analysis, place her firmly among the holy men and women of the Church.

In Davis' analysis, these five black people were similar in many ways, but it is their humility that makes them most distinctive. He compared true humility, as compared with false, ascribed humility.

> Humility is the favorite virtue that a dominant group wishes to ascribe to saintly representatives of the oppressed. ... 'Humility' insures that the oppressed remember their subordinate position. This kind of humility – a travesty of the true virtue – never seems to be attested to by the sources nearest to the saint. Humility is the result of one's encounter with God. Only in His presence are we conscious of our nothingness. But for the Christian this is never the whole reality – for it is the Word Incarnate that makes this mortal dust something glorious.[41]

The five black men and woman that Davis described have at their core an aspect of quiet contemplation. In his recent book, *The Sovereignty of Quiet – Beyond Resistance in Black Culture*, Kevin Quashie contrasts the power of quiet contemplation with the more common trend to see blackness through a more public sociocultural lens of resistance.

> The praying subject explores the inner life, encounters and tries to give name to desires and vulnerabilities. One waits, waits to see one's own self revealed, to feel the range of sentiments that manifest when one sits and

---

[41] Davis, "Spirituality," 99-100.

waits. This waiting is tingly and it can momentarily liberate the self from the strictures of its social identity.[42]

The conflict described by Quashie is the same conflict that Davis described – true interiority as opposed to the ascription of a resistance that must be controlled.

Edward Braxton was offered the distinction of summing up the key points of the meeting in a concluding essay. He made a series of remarks that seem almost prescient for the time. He called for ongoing collaboration, and noted the skilled work done by women scholars at the meeting, writing that "Black Catholic women doing scholarship on questions specifically related to the Catholic community is of great value and great urgency."[43] He insisted that the work done during that historic meeting in 1978 needed to be chronicled. Braxton insisted:

> Some of us must do something. I would suggest that some of us or each of us, in our own way and style and with whatever degree of time and energy we have is to [sic] chronicle what we are about. Aware that we are at a peculiar juncture in history we must record it! Whatever the context of our ministry, we should chronicle it. This will be a valuable account of a turning point in American culture and the Church.
>
> Unless we start chronicling what we are doing, something valuable will be lost. Ten or fifteen years from now someone will say, "Oh, yes, remember when we first met, who was at that meeting?" "Who first began to adapt the Catholic liturgy to various black contexts?" "What were the issues? Areas of consensus and conflict?"[44]

Finally, he pointed out that the work of changing the culture of the American Church would be difficult. It would require serious, challenging dialogue – dialogue that allows all those who are serious about change to grow in "a collective process."[45]

The 1978 meeting of Black Catholic scholars and the subsequent publication of *Theology: A Portrait in Black* was historic and

---

[42] Kevin Quashie, *The Sovereignty of Quiet – Beyond Resistance in Black Culture* (New Jersey: Rutgers University Press, 2012), 113.
[43] Edward Braxton, "Concluding Reflections," *Theology: A Portrait in Black*, (Pittsburgh, PA: Capuchin Press, 1980), 161-167, quote from page 161.
[44] Braxton, "Concluding Reflections", 164.
[45] Braxton, "Concluding Reflections," 167.

foundational. The seeds that were planted then germinated and have borne rich fruit. Following the second meeting of the group, there was a decade-long hiatus of the scholarly symposium. During that time, Thaddeus Posey turned his attention toward the creation of the Institute for Black Catholic Studies at Xavier University. He served as co-director for the next decade. In the 35 years since its inception, the Institute graduated more than 68 men and women with masters' degrees in theology.[46] *Theology: A Portrait in Black* was used for that first decade as a source book for the students, and continues to inform their ministry to this day.

Of the thirty-three charter members who met in Baltimore in 1978, many went on to earn doctoral degrees and have been actively engaging in scholarship, teaching, and ministry. Four have been appointed bishops – Moses Anderson, S.S.E., Edward Braxton, Terry Steib, S.V.D., and Joseph Perry. The scholarly group re-convened in 1991 as the Black Catholic Theological Symposium under the leadership of Jamie Phelps and Shawn Copeland, and in 2007 established its own scholarly peer-reviewed journal, published annually – *The Journal of the Black Catholic Theological Symposium*. In the thirty-five years since its publication, *Theology: A Portrait in Black* inspired hundreds of individuals, thereby helping set the American Church on a path toward inclusion. In many ways, it was both a product of its time and a beacon of hope for all those with a passion for brotherhood, sisterhood, and justice.

---

[46]Vanessa White, "Thirty Years of Impact: The Institute for Black Catholic Studies," *The Journal of the Black Catholic Theological Symposium* IV (2010):17-19, esp. page 17.

Works Cited

Bellow, Kathleen Dorsey. "The Black Community and the Call for Vatican Council II (1962-1965)," *The Journal of the Black Catholic Theological Symposium* VIII (2014): 21-53, quote from page 24.

Braxton, Edward. "Concluding Reflections," *Theology: A Portrait in Black*, (Pittsburgh, PA: Capuchin Press, 1980), 161-167.

Braxton, Edward. "Religion, Values, Ethnicity, and the Black Experience," *Theology: A Portrait in Black*, (Pittsburgh, PA: Capuchin Press, 1980), 15-30.

Clark, Kenneth B., Isidor Chein, and Stuart W. Cook, "The Effects of Segregation and the Consequences of Desegregation, A {September 1952) Social Science Statement in the Brown v. Board of Education of Topeka Supreme Court Case," reprinted in *American Psychologist* 59 (September 2004): 495-501.

Cleage, Albert. *Black Christian Nationalism: New Directions for the Black Church* (New York: W. Morrow, 1972), xxv –xxvi.

Coates, James. "Riots Follow Killing of Martin Luther King, Jr.," *Chicago Tribune*, December 19, 2007, accessed October 10, 2014.

Culver, Virginina. "People Watch Black Priest," *The Denver Post*, December 21, 1973.

Davis, Cyprian. "Spirituality," *Theology: A Portrait in Black*, (Pittsburgh, PA: Capuchin Press, 1980).

Davis, Cyprian. "To Be Both Black and Catholic," *Marianist Award Lecture 2006* (The University of Dayton, 2007).

Davis, Cyprian and Jamie Phelps. *Stamped in the Image of God, African Americans as God's Image in Black* (Maryknoll, NY: Orbis Books).

Decree *Ad Gentes* on the Mission Activity of the Church, From the Vatican Archives web site, accessed January 2, 2014, http://www.vatican.va/archive/hist_councils/ii_vatican_council/index.htm.

Dickens, Charles. *A Tale of Two Cities* (New York: Dover Thrift Editions, 1999).

Dogmatic Constitution of the Church, *Lumen Gentium*, Solemnly Promulgated by His Holiness Pope Paul VI on November 21, 1964.

From the Vatican Archives web site, accessed December 30, 2013, http://www.vatican.va/archive/hist_councils/ii_vatican_council/index.htm.

Franklin, V.P. "Introduction: Brown v. Board of Education: Fifty Years of Educational Change in the United States," *The Journal of African American History* 90, No. 1/2, Brown v. Board of Education: Fifty Years of Educational Change in the United States, 1954-2004, (2005): 1-8.

Gadsden, Brett. "'He Said He Wouldn't Help Me Get a Jim Crow Bus': The Shifting Terms of the Challenge to Segregated Public Education, 1950-1954", *The Journal of African American History, vol. 90, No. 1/2, Brown v. Board of Education: Fifty Years of Educational Change in the United States, 1954-2004* (2005): 9-28.

Harris, Elbert. "Issues Concerning the Development of the Catholic Church in the Black Community," *Theology: A Portrait in Black*, (Pittsburgh, PA: Capuchin Press, 1980), 126-131.

"John XXIII: The Speech to the Moon Above ... ", News.VA, Official Vatican Network, accessed September 14, 2016, http://saltandlighttv.org/blogfeed/getpost.php?id=41290&language=en Salt + Light Media.

Kerr, David. "Pilgrims Crowd Bl. John XXIII's Grave On Day He Died," *Catholic News Agency*, June 3, 2011, From Catholic News Agency web site, http://www.catholicnewsagency.com (accessed October 24, 2014). See also, "Look Ahead, Pontiff Advises Young Inmates," *St. Petersburg Times, Associated Press*, November 12, 1962, accessed January 2, 2014.

Lackner, Joseph. "Dan A. Rudd, Editor of the American Catholic Tribune, From Bardstown to Cincinnati," *Catholic Historical Review* 80, No. 2 (1994): 258-281.

McKnight, Albert. "A Black Christian Perspective on Spirituality," *Theology: A Portrait in Black*, (Pittsburgh, PA: Capuchin Press, 1980), 103-112.

Moore, Cecilia. "Victor and Constance Daniel and Emancipatory Education at the Cardinal Gibbons Institute," *Journal of Catholic Education* 4[3] (2001): 396-404.

Moore, Cecilia and Kimberly Flint-Hamilton, "Cyprian Davis, O.S.B.: To Walk a Path, To Be Transformed, and To Transform," *The Journal of the Black Catholic Theological Symposium*, vol. IV (2010): 29-56.

Nearon, Joseph. "A Challenge to Theology: The Situation of American Blacks," *Proceedings of the Catholic Theological Society of America* 30 (1975): 177-202, esp. page 183; Joseph Nearon, "Introduction," *Theology, A Portrait in Black*, (Pittsburgh, PA: Capuchin Press, 1980).

Phelps, Jamie. "Black Self-Concept," *Theology: A Portrait in Black*, (Pittsburgh, PA: Capuchin Press, 1980), 52-65.

Pope John XXIII, "Opening Speech for Council of Vatican II," October 11, 1962, The Second Vatican Ecumenical Council , Vatican II, Papal Encyclicals Online, accessed October 20, 2014, http://www.papalencyclicals.net/vatican2.htm.

Pope John XXIII. *Pacem in Terris*, as quoted *in Social Justice: The Catholic Position*, ed. Vincent P. Mainelli (Washington, D.C.: Consortium Press, 1975), #309.

Pope Paul VI, *Populorum Progresso*, as quoted in *Social Justice: The Catholic Position*, ed. Vincent P. Mainelli (Washington, D.C.: Consortium Press, 1967), #866, 867, 868.

Quashie, Kevin. *The Sovereignty of Quiet – Beyond Resistance in Black Culture* (New Jersey: Rutgers University Press, 2012).

Raboteau, Albert. "Relating Race and Religion, Four Historical Models," in *Uncommon Faithfulness: The Black Catholic Experience*, ed. M. Shawn Copeland (Maryknoll, NY: Orbis Books, 2009), 9-25.

Rivers, Clarence. "Thank God We Ain't What We Was: The State of the Liturgy in the Black Catholic Community," *Theology: A Portrait in Black*, (Pittsburgh, PA: Capuchin Press, 1980), 66-74.

White, Vanessa. "Thirty Years of Impact: The Institute for Black Catholic Studies," *The Journal of the Black Catholic Theological Symposium* IV (2010): 17-19.

Woodson, Carter B. *The Mis-Education of the Negro*, (New York: Dover edition, 2005 [1933]), ix-x.

"Just Enough"

A Poem by Steve Hamilton

How much love does it take
To forgive someone's mistake?
If there was a sign from above
It would say, "Just Enough."

Why must a child go to sleep
Crying out for food to eat?
Deprivation; the education he thinks of,
When all he needs is just enough.

How much love, would you say,
Could have saved the life of Freddie Gray?
He didn't have to die riding rough
If there had been just enough.

Unarmed black men gunned down in the street.
Process due denied, blatantly.
Ask yourself, "If it's not just enough for me,
Is it justice that I see?"
How could it be?

Love's a pure and simple gift, an action, word, a thought,
To help another's life along the way.
Love is free to everyone, it never could be bought.
We get it back when we give it away.

How much love does it take
Before we can conquer fear and hate?
If there was a sign from above
It would say, "Just Enough."

So, how will we right all of our wrongs?
And, why must it take so very long?
A heard a man sing, "All You Need Is Love"
Just Enough... Just Enough... Just Enough...
Love.

The Risk of Memory, The Cost of Forgetting[1]

Dr. M. Shawn Copeland
Boston College
Chestnut Hill, Massachusetts

> Not everything that is faced can be changed,
> but nothing can be changed until it is faced.
> James Baldwin
>
> If we can truly remember, they will not forget.
> Miller Williams, "Of History and Hope"

Abstract: This article focuses on the risk of memory and the cost of forgetting. Memory, and the act of remembering both individually and collectively as a society, involves risk to a society's present, past, and future. Forgetting comes at a price exacted by the past, but paid in the present for the future, even as nations sometimes choose to forget. This thesis is developed in three parts – common meaning and memory as grounding a community; the cost of forgetting so as to erase memory of wrongdoing; and the terrible implications of the cost of forgetting in the context of the shooting at Mother Emmanuel African Methodist Episcopal (AME) Church on June 17, 2015 in South Carolina. When we risk memory, we collectively take responsibility to embody ethical responsibility for the past, in the present, and for the future.

Keywords: Memory, forgetting, forgiveness, reconciliation, shooting

Memory makes us who we are; it provides fixed points by which to take our bearings, to steer our lives. To lose memory is to look with indifference on those whom we have cherished and loved, to misplace treasured possessions, to disregard valuable experience. In the *Philebus*, Socrates says to Protarchus, "If you had no memory you could not even remember that you ever did enjoy pleasure, and no recollection whatever of present pleasure could remain with you" (Plato, *Philebus* 21c). Without memory, time present, time future, and time past fuse. Without memory, a spouse or lover, friend or relative, daughter or son is simply a face, an interesting face, perhaps, but strange and unknown.

---

[1] This is a revision of the Raymund Schwager, S.J., Memorial Lecture, given at the Colloquium on Religion and Violence, July 10, 2015, Saint Louis University, St. Louis, Missouri.

To lose memory is to lose, in large measure, capacities to understand, to make sense out of what is happening, to make meaning. Amnesia or Alzheimer's disease sadden and frighten us, because memory is tied so closely to identity. To lose memory is to lose oneself.

Yet, the power of memory may not always be so salutary or benign. Memories of war or genocide, of interrogation or torture, of physical or sexual assault induce anxious, confused, and conflicting responses. Perhaps, a necessary suppression of memory functions to safeguard psychic health, for when traumatic memories swim up into consciousness, dreams bleed into nightmares often inducing "literal return" of the event against the will of the suffering individual.[2]

Memory, individual or personal as well as common or shared, is an intentional and selective act. It sorts and categorizes, erases and embellishes, conceals and reveals. And, "While memory requires time to become what it is, time also hinders memory."[3] Memory may fade, may be filtered or altered or manipulated. Forgetting is the opposite of memory. Forgetting includes *both* unintentional failures to notice something or someone *and* intentional acts of erasure or deletion of what once was known.[4] Perhaps, unintentional forgetting holds some practical utility, preventing us from an overload of minutiae or distractions that could prove detrimental to well being. On the other hand, forgetting as an intentional and active "strategy of avoidance, evasion, [or] flight entails the same sort of responsibility as that imputed to acts of negligence, omission, imprudence, [and] lack of foresight."[5]

For religion and politics, memory and forgetting raise serious, even, ontological questions. Within these two powerful spheres of

---

[2] Cathy Caruth, "Trauma and Experience," 200, in *Theories of Memory: A Reader*. Eds. Michael Rossington and Anne Whitehead (Baltimore: The Johns Hopkins University Press, 2007); see also, Edward S. Casey, *Remembering: A Phenomenological Study* 2nd ed (Bloomington and Indianapolis: Indiana University Press, 2000), xiii. "The 'return of the repressed' in symptoms and dreams is itself opaque in its significance; the why of their appearance is mysterious and hence calls for active interpretation. The highly encrypted character of what returns signifies that it is riddled with forgetting; the façade of symptom or dream is oblivious to its origins," xiii.
[3] Gerhard Richter, "Acts of Memory and Mourning: Derrida and the Fictions of Anteriority," 150, in *Memory, History, Theories, and Debates*, eds. Susannah Radstone and Bill Schwarz (New York: Fordham University Press, 2010).
[4] Miroslav Volf, *The End of Memory* (Grand Rapids, Michigan / Cambridge, U.K.: William B. Eerdmans Publishing Company, 2006), 145.
[5] Paul Ricoeur, *Memory, History, Forgetting*, trans. Kathleen Blamey and David Pellauer (Chicago and London: University of Chicago Press, 2004), 449.

human life, common memory possesses an ethical function: the *mnemonic* act must be undertaken seriously and rigorously, must be open to past and future, to reverence and lament, to punishment and reparation—and above all, in religion, to transcendence. The *mnemonic* act binds as well as releases, strengthens as well as debilitates, deconstructs as well as reconstructs.

By clarifying the practical-political (and mystical) implications of *anamnesis*, of the *dangerous memory* of the passion and death of the Crucified Jewish Jesus for the practice of Christian faith, Johann Baptist Metz confronted the covert corrosive intermingling of politics and religion. He uncovered the fateful memory of German complicity and cooperation at individual, communal, cultural, social, and religious levels with the Nazi attempt to destroy the Jewish people. At the same time, Metz pointed up technical rationality's obsession with short-term goals and refusal to reflect upon the long-term implications of its decisions. Metz showed that what is at stake in the competition of the furtive, fast, and furious is the casual *forgetfulness* of the Body of Jesus of Nazareth, *forgetfulness* of the bodies "piled up"[6] by force and expropriation, coercion and cruelty. The Christian exercise of memory purports to be radically different: Christian memory seeks to challenge and transform the perspectives and *praxis* of believers, for at the heart of Christian memory lies the broken body of Christ; Christian discipleship requires imitation of Him.

My overall concerns here are the social implications of common or shared memory.[7] My thesis argues that memory (remembering) involves risk to a society's present, past, and future, *and* that forgetting comes at a price exacted by the past, but paid in the present for the future. Still, memory may pose so burdensome a risk that a nation *chooses to forget*; yet, that very *forgetting* presents a formidable obstacle to healing and reconciliation, and, thereby, jeopardizes that nation's present and future. I will elaborate this in *three parts*: The *first part* considers common meaning and common memory as grounding community in support of creating a nation, then, develops *collective taking*

---

[6] Johann Baptist Metz, *Faith in History and Society: Toward a Practical Fundamental Theology*, trans. J. Matthew Ashley (1992; New York: Crossroad Publishing Company, 2007), 101.

[7] The terms collective memory, common or shared memory may convey different, even conflicting, meanings as these are posed by different theorists. I use these terms here to my own purpose, but my basic understanding and use of the notion of common memory draws on the work of philosopher and theologian Bernard Lonergan in *Method in Theology* (New York: Herder & Herder, 1972).

responsibility as a central risk in bringing collective or national wrongdoing to the foreground of common memory. The *second part* probes the *cost of forgetting* as a nation wrestles with attempts to erase memory of wrongdoing. The *third part* gestures toward the most heartbreaking implications of the risk of *common memory* and the *cost of forgetting* as these converge in the horrific shooting of Sharonda Coleman-Singleton, DePayne Middleton Doctor, Cynthia Hurd, Susie Jackson, Ethel Lance, Clementa Pinckney, Tywanza Sanders, Daniel Simmons, and Myra Thompson at Mother Emanuel African Methodist Episcopal (AME) Church on June 17, 2015 in Charleston, South Carolina.[8] My focus on the deaths of these nine women and men ought not to be taken that imply that I am unconcerned or unmoved by the deaths of black and brown women and men in police custody or at the hands of police or of their designated associates as in the cases of Trayvon Martin and Eric Harris.[9] Certainly, the deaths of Eric Garner in Staten Island, New York, Michael Brown in Ferguson, Missouri, Tamir Rice in Cleveland, Ohio, Walter Scott in North Charleston, South Carolina, Freddie Gray in Baltimore, Maryland, Sandra Bland in Waller County, Texas, Aiyana Stanley-Jones in Detroit, Reika Boyd in Chicago, Andy Lopez in Santa Rosa, California, Akai Gurley in Brooklyn, New York, John Crawford III in Beavercreek, Ohio, Ezell Ford in Los Angeles, California, *must never be forgotten*. These deaths denote loss of human life, the murder of human persons—a spouse, a daughter or son, a grandchild or grandparent, an aunt or uncle, a niece or nephew, a cousin or friend. These deaths manifest a most egregious breakdown of humane values in our culture and the collapse of the system of criminal

---

[8] The Reverend Norvel Goff, a presiding elder of the 7th District AME Church in South Carolina, was reported as saying, "The blood of the 'Mother Emmanuel 9' requires us to work until not only justice in this case, but for those who are still living in the margin of life, those who are less fortunate than ourselves," http://www.cbsnews.com/news/charleston-shooting-emanuel-african-methodist-episcopal-church-hosts-first-sunday-services-since.Although it well may be too soon to write dispassionately and adequately about this terrible event, as a practicing Christian and a theologian, for me to pass over this event would be *immoral*; as an African American woman, surely the descendant of enslaved Africans, to do so would be *impious*; as a citizen of the United States of America, it would be *irresponsible*; as a scholar, it would be *cowardly*.

[9] Trayvon Martin was shot to death on February 26, 2012, in Sanford, Florida, by George Zimmerman, a neighborhood watch captain for the gated community in which Martin was visiting. Zimmerman was charged with and tried for second-degree murder, but was acquitted on all counts. Eric Harris was shot to death on April 2, 2015 in Tulsa, Oklahoma, by Reserve Deputy Robert Bates, who allegedly reached for his taser but instead pulled out a gun. Bates was charged with second-degree manslaughter involving culpable negligence.

justice in the United States.[10] *These women and men and youth must never be forgotten.*

THE RISK OF COMMON MEMORY

All memories, Maurice Halbwachs maintains, are communal. Individuals do not remember *alone*, but rather "as members of a group."[11] It is within families, friendships, and associations, within communities, within societies "that people normally acquire their memories" and here, too, women and men "recall, recognize, and localize their memories."[12] Common or shared memory requires and grounds community, and while shared geography may be important, it is not the formal determinant of community—*common meaning is*. Community is achievement of common meaning: Common meaning entails shared or analogous, even, plural experience, common and complementary understanding, judgment, decision, and action. Common meaning is realized in communal choices and decisions, in embrace of common values, goals, policies, commitments, and loves. "Community coheres or divides, begins or ends, just where the common field of experience, common understanding, common judgment, common commitments begin and end."[13]

---

[10] See William J. Stuntz, *The Collapse of American Criminal Justice* (Cambridge, MA: The Belknap Press of Harvard University, 2011) and Michelle Alexander, *The New Jim Crow: Mass Incarceration in the Age of Colorblindness* (New York: The New Press, 2010).
[11] Maurice Halbwachs, *The Collective Memory* (New York: Harper-Colophon Books, 1950), 48. There is considerable debate over the role of individual agency in Halbwachs' notion of collective memory. Paul Ricoeur observes, "it was in the personal act of recollection that the mark of the social was initially sought and found,"(*Memory, History, Forgetting*: 123). Further he points out that Halbwachs' belief that collective memory is inflected by the individual's relationship with different groups opens up the very possibility for individual agency, because Halbwachs provides "every consciousness with the power to place itself within the viewpoint of the group and, in addition, to move from one group to another" (Ibid). Jan Assmann is critical of Halbwachs' distinction between history and memory in not seeming to take into systematic account of those collective memories that extend beyond the span or range of a lifetime. Assmann distinguishes between 'communicative memory' and 'cultural memory' noting the latter's concern for the distant past and dependence upon specialized practice of transmission.
[12] Halbwachs, "The Social Frameworks of Memory," in his *On Collective Memory*, ed. and trans. Lewis A. Coser (Chicago: University of Chicago Press, 1992), 38, 52-53, 171-173.
[13] Lonergan, *Method in Theology*, 79.

Because a world of different and differentiated experiences and their meanings ranges well beyond any individual's immediate or personal experience, a community and a nation cultivates common memory—sifting, collating, and making available differing and differentiated experiences, expressions, products, and memories of individual and collective understanding, judgment, and action. Common memory conserves and communicates a common past; nurtures a common present, and fashions a common future. Yet, achievement, preservation, and transmission of common memory are neither simple, nor simplistic; in this endeavor, historical memory and critical history are indispensable.

What does it mean to remember—to remember collective or group or social trauma? In recent decades, we have come to understand memory of traumatic experience, particularly, collective or group experience, such as slavery, genocide, internment, ethnic cleansing, hate crimes, feminicide, torture, disappearance, and mass atrocities as a political act. Mari Ruti argues, "an excess of memory may be paralyzing, impeding the emergence of new modalities of life, of new passions, possibilities, and preoccupations."[14] What does it mean to remember—to remember collective or group wrongdoing and how should such wrongdoing be remembered? Public acts of grieving, official apologies, reparations as well as commemorative efforts through museums, monuments, and artistic interventions remain morally and ethically necessary.[15] And, although repression of facts of wrongdoing and violent events may provoke imitation in subsequent generations, immersion in or fascination with narratives of victimization could lead to repetition of those acts or corrosive bitterness or self-wounding.

A nation that remembers wrongs it has committed against subjugated groups or peoples or even oppression wielded against its own citizens in the past, *risks responsibility*. Indeed, for a nation to risk the *collective taking responsibility* for past wrongs stands as a daunting task and cannot be undertaken grudgingly or half-heartedly or under threat. Certainly, collective taking responsibility for past wrongs cannot undo the harm or minimize the gravity, but undertaking such action,

---

[14] Mari Ruti, "Is Autonomy Unethical? Trauma and the Politics of Responsibility," 51, in *The Ethics of Remembering and the Consequences of Forgetting: Essays on Trauma, History, and Memory*, ed. Michael O'Loughlin (Lanham: Rowman & Littlefield, 2015).
[15] Ruti, "Is Autonomy Unethical? Trauma and the Politics of Responsibility," 51, in *The Ethics of Remembering and the Consequences of Forgetting*, 51.

Jeffrey Blustein insists, does effect, "a retroactive change in the significance of the past wrongdoing."[16] The wrongdoing now is invested with different meaning "because it is acknowledged *as* wrong and responsibility is taken for it."[17] To quote Blustein again:

> by accepting the burden of making amends, the responsible group demonstrates its willingness to accept some pain and humiliation for the sake of the victims and, in do doing, symbolically asserts what was previously denied, namely the moral standing of the victims."[18]

Collective taking responsibility for collective wrongs involves three interrelated and socially significant imperatives—*cognitive, affective, and moral*. The *cognitive demand* requires much more than some vague awareness of past wrong, but rather critical and sympathetic inquiry, learning, and understanding. Certainly, this entails an apprenticeship to history as a guide in "discerning and telling the truth about certain events and people in the past."[19] The *affective* calls for engagement with and reorientation of the emotions, for historical explanation alone cannot overcome fear or alienation or shame at wrongdoing or at having been wronged. Through interpersonal encounter, conversation, structured group dialogues, and heightened attention to intersubjectivity hearts may be opened and changed. The *moral imperative* moves a nation's people to action. *Collective taking responsibility* involves moral encounter with festering wounds and foreclosed grievances—neither to appease a wronged group, nor simply mourn these wrongs and render them static, "but to militate on behalf of them."[20] To risk responsibility is to risk *action for change*; *merely* calling to mind evil committed will not remedy evil.

THE COST OF FORGETTING

After the collapse of destructive and violent regimes, Germany, Spain, Chile, Argentina, and South Africa, Paul Connerton suggests,

---

[16] Jeffrey Blustein, *The Moral Demands of Memory* (Cambridge: Cambridge University Press, 2008), 142-143
[17] Blustein, *The Moral Demands of Memory* 142-143
[18] Blustein, *The Moral Demands of Memory*, 142-143.
[19] Blustein, *The Moral Demands of Memory*, 212.
[20] Sara Kaplan, "Souls at the Crossroads, Africans on the Water: The Politics of Diasporic Melancholia," *Callaloo*, Vol. 30, No. 2 (Spring 2007): 511-526 at 521.

"needed to take up some explicit position with regard to that past."[21] Publications of personal testimonies about experiences of torture and oppression carried out under these totalitarian regimes have given rise to the notion of an "ethics of memory."[22] Although, forgetting may not necessarily be unethical, forgetting "forced upon human beings against their will or interest"[23] *most certainly is.* Let us consider two types of coerced forgetting: *repressive erasure* and *structural amnesia*.

States, governments, or ruling parties utilize *repressive erasure* to deny historical events or facts, crucial ruptures or breaks.[24] Turkish denial and dismissal of the Armenian charge of genocide provides one example of this type of forgetting. The lack of an apology from the United States federal government to the indigenous peoples for expropriation of land and violation of treaties presents still another.

Repressive erasure also may be covert. Through "spatial script[ing]"[25] and editing, curators of museums and galleries, designers and architects of public spaces establish "iconographic programmes" that highlight what is or is not of political and aesthetic significance. "In exhibiting a master narrative, the museum's spatial script is overt in its acts of celebratory remembrance, covert in acts of editing out and erasure."[26] Consider Richmond, Virginia's Monument Avenue with its statues of Confederate Generals Stonewall Jackson, Robert E. Lee, and Jeb Stuart; Confederate Naval Officer Matthew Maury, and Confederate President Jefferson Davis;[27] contrast this with the asphalt parking lot that has covered over the historic "Burial Ground for Negroes."[28] Achille Mbembe points us toward the "sinister significations" of such

---

[21] Paul Connerton, *The Spirit of Mourning* (Cambridge: Cambridge University Press, 2011), 33. Connerton wonders whether forgetting is necessarily a failing. He distinguishes three types of forgetting that "establish and enhance social bonds: forgetting as prescriptive, as constitutive in formation of new identity, and as annulment.
[22] Connerton, *The Spirit of Mourning* 34; some such testimonies come from Elie Wiesel, Primo Levi, Jacobo Timerman, and Alexander Solzhenitsyn.
[23] Connerton, *The Spirit of Mourning*, 40.
[24] Connerton, *The Spirit of Mourning*, 41.
[25] Connerton, *The Spirit of Mourning*, 41.
[26] Connerton, *The Spirit of Mourning*, 41.
[27] Reportedly a statue to the late Virginia native and tennis great Arthur Ashe has been erected on Monument Avenue. But consider the *weight* of such a commemorative statue in relation to the social and cultural power of white racist supremacy.
[28] Michael Kranish, "Remembrance of Crimes Past," *The Boston Sunday Globe*, July 5, 2015, A7.

monuments."[29] For those white men and women who embrace the dominative whiteness of US culture such "commemorative" monuments not only participate in but also sustain "heroic narratives of domination" and literally reinscribe and reinforce ongoing white supremacy and arbitrary power.[30]

John Barnes employed the phrase *structural amnesia* in his genealogical studies to explain the suppression of suspect matrilineal lines in mapping the British peerage,[31] but it resonates with the notion of *structural embarrassment*. Coined by historian of religions Charles H. Long, *structural embarrassment* constitutes one way to describe the relationship of the descendants of the enslaved Africans to the U. S. population. Certainly, a segment of our population can claim descent from the seventeenth century European (British and French, in particular) settlers; a large and increasing larger group identifies their descent from political refugees or immigrants and, indeed, are global immigrants themselves; and a small number of people may claim indigenous status. Then, there are the 'dark others;' from whence do they come?

How is a courageous and thoughtful, fractious and slaveholding group of men (and women) who, inspired by European Enlightenment ideals, revolted from a tyrannical colonizing power in order to gain political and economic freedom, committed their lives and sacred honor to uphold certain inalienable rights of life, liberty, and untrammeled pursuit of happiness, to pass on through history to their political descendants these values—despite the subjugation of a people, despite the legalization of black *unfreedom*? How is a nation so conceived and so dedicated to liberty and to equality *to acknowledge* and *confess* to a history of slaveholding—*on its own territory*? Its people *turn away from the offending knowledge; gloss over and fudge historical fact; conceal and hide from the very truths they conceal.*

Slavery is the "tough stuff of American memory."[32] We conspire to forget, we repress or edit; we delete our knowledge. Scholarly and

---

[29] Cited in Elaine Coburn, "*Critique de la raison Nègre*: A Review," in *Decolonization, Indigeneity, Education & Society* Vol. 3, No. 2 (2014): 185.
[30] Cited in Elaine Coburn, "*Critique de la Raison Nègre*: A Review," in *Decolonization, Indigeneity, Education & Society* Vol. 3, No. 2 (2014): 185.
[31] Connerton, *The Spirit of Mourning*, 44.
[32] James Oliver and Lois E. Horton, eds. *Slavery and Public History: The Tough Stuff of American Memory* (Chapel Hill: University of North Carolina Press, 2006); see Thomas McCarthy, "*Vergangenheitsbewältigung* in the USA: On the Politics of the Memory of Slavery," *Political Theory*, Vol. 30, No,5 (October 2002): 623-648.

popular interest in slavery is of recent vintage, notes historian Ira Berlin, and dates from the last years of the twentieth century and the initial years of the twenty-first.[33] Americans are neither exceptional, nor alone in the effort to repress national exploitation, violence, and evil. William Stanner coined the term 'The Great Australian Silence' to critique the persistent refusals of the Australian government to apologize to the aboriginal people for a century (1869-1969) of forcible removal of their children from their families.[34]

Repressive erasure does not mean that there are no individual members of a dominant culture or group who lack remorse or feel the wrench of conscience when contemplating the damage and destruction done to indigenous peoples or descendants of enslaved or marginalized and minoritized peoples. Rather, this form of forgetting progressively and systematically erases the achievements or contributions or experiences of these groups from common and national memory.

What does a community, a nation *forfeit* when it repressively erases memory of the very presence and condition of those whom they have dishonored, when it overlooks and humiliates those groups into silence and invisibility? Remembering *is* terrifying, especially when the perpetrators of wrong are no longer available, when death and decades disrupt the possibility of apology or direct reparations to survivors. How does a nation restore to a subjugated and oppressed people their languages and ceremonies, their lands and cultures, their hopes and dreams?

No reparations can suffice. But James Baldwin contends, "Not everything that is faced can be changed, but nothing can be changed until it is faced." Traumatic wrongs like genocide and slavery wield a body blow to "social life and damages the bonds linking people together and impairs the prevailing sense of community."[35] *By forgetting* its past, a nation relinquishes *social integrity* as well as *authentic moral integrity*

---

[33] Ira Berlin, "Coming to Terms with Slavery in Twenty-First Century America," 1, in *Slavery and Public History: The Tough Stuff of American History*.

[34] See William Edward Hanley Stanner, *After the Dreaming* (19601, 1968). Robert Manne, "The Sorry History of Australia's Apology"
http://www.theguardian.com/commentisfree/2013/may/26/sorry-history-australia-apology-indigenous/ On February 12, 2008, the Australian Parliament issued a formal apology to the Aboriginal people; on the following day, in a formal, public ceremony Prime Minister Kevin Rudd apologized.

[35] Ricardo C. Ainslie, "Trauma, Community, and Contemporary Racial Violence: Reflections on the Architecture of Memory," 313, in *The Ethics of Remembering and the Consequences of Forgetting*.

and *authority*. Moreover, *by forgetting* its past, a nation risks its unity or cohesion, its very moral existence.

FORGIVENESS

This third and final section reflects briefly on forgiveness in relation to the shooting at Mother Emanuel AME Church in June 2015. That nine black women and men were shot to death *because of their race*, and that the shooter would express himself in terms of white supremacy reminds us (to adapt a phrase by Michael Ignatieff) the past continues to trouble us because it is *not* past.[36] For René Girard collective persecutions denote "acts of violence committed directly by a mob of murderers such as the persecution of the Jews during the Black Death;" collective resonances refer to "acts of violence, such as witch-hunts, that are legal in form but stimulated by the extremes of public opinion."[37] In the United States, the lynching of blacks meets the criteria of collective persecution;[38] arguably, the shooting at Mother Emanuel AME Church approximates the intent and meaning of collective resonances of persecution. The shooting was an act of violence, *illegal* under the laws of the State of South Carolina and the laws of the United States of America. This shooting registers as a hate crime.[39] But, even more alarmingly, this hate crime was enacted within a cultural horizon that honors and postures the putative legitimacy of white supremacy; the political dimension of this violence was enhanced by the perpetrator's explicit adherence to the insolent memorial and ensign of sedition, the Confederate flag.

---

[36] Michael Ignatieff, "The Elusive Goal of War Trials," *Harper's*, March 1996, reprinted in "Articles of Faith, Index on Censorship," *Harper's*, September/October 1997, 15, 16-17. Cited in Martha Minow, *Between Vengeance and Forgiveness* (Boston: Beacon Press, 1998), 13.
[37] René Girard, *The Scapegoat,* trans. Yvonne Freccero (Baltimore: The Johns Hopkins University Press, 1986), 12.
[38] Lynching was a capricious instrument of terror exercised by Northern and Southern whites. Between the end of the Civil War and 1968, ordinary white men and women, tacitly or actively, legitimated the lynching of more than five thousand black men and women. The alleged reasons for lynching blacks included homicide, assault, robbery and theft; but the grounding reasons for lynching were insult to whites, rape, and attempted rape. Most basically, however, lynching sought to maintain white dominance or supremacy, to monitor and control the boundaries of racial caste and class.
[39] Legally defined a hate crime is a crime motivated by racial, religious, gender, sexual orientation, or other prejudice.

The Confederate battle flag endures as one of the most persistent and provocative memorial-symbols of the slaveholding South. South Carolinians, both black and white, have protested since it was raised over the state house in 1962 in defiance of desegregation. In 2002 the flag was removed from atop the state house to a pole set up in front of it—still protests continued. After the shooting, photographs of Dylann Roof made public depicted him holding the Confederate battle flag.

After the murders, protests to remove the flag increased and sharpened. On June 22, 2015, South Carolina Governor Nikki Haley called the South Carolina Legislature to take up removal of the flag. On June, 27, 2015, Bree Newsome climbed the flagpole and took down the flag; immediately, she was arrested. During a rally in the wake of the shooting, Michaela Pilar Brown, a Columbia artist said, "We know what that flag symbolizes. We know the hate. We know the danger. It says 'stop.' It says 'you are not welcome here.' It says 'fear for your life.' Take down the flag."[40] The South Carolina legislature voted to remove the flag and it was taken down with conspicuous ceremony on July 10, 2015.

Dylann Roof sought out white supremacists, whether virtually or actually, who packaged and sold hatred and its symbols as heritage, as tradition, as common memory of white supremacy. In defense of that heritage, tradition, and memory, Roof aimed to ignite a race war between blacks and whites, to purge his community of so-called impure and corrupting elements.[41]

That his vicious act failed to accomplish its evil purpose (violent contagion) may be attributed surely to the *Black Christian Principle*: that is, the unwavering belief treasured, taught, and reiterated by *all* black Christian churches—that *all* human beings are made in the image and likeness of God, that *all* human beings are creatures of inestimable

---

[40] http://www.cbsnews.com/news/charleston-shooting-emanuel-african-methodist-episcopal-church-hosts-first-sunday-services-since/ The South Carolina legislature voted to remove the flag and it was taken down on July 10, 2015.

[41] Roof wrote in an alleged manifesto, "I have no choice. I am not in the position to, alone, go into the ghetto and fight. I chose Charleston because it is most historic city in my state, and at one time had the highest ratio of blacks to Whites in the country," http://www.cbsnews.com/news/charleston-shooting-emanuel-african-methodist-episcopal-church-hosts-first-sunday-services-since/. About the Confederate Flag, Michaela Pilar Brown, a Columbia artist said at a protest rally "We know what that flag symbolizes. We know the hate. We know the danger. It says 'stop.' It says 'you are not welcome here.' It says 'fear for your life.' Take down the flag" http://www.cbsnews.com/news/charleston-shooting-emanuel-african-methodist-episcopal-church-hosts-first-sunday-services-since/

dignity and worth, and that life is precious and sacred. Family members of the murdered women and men offered the murderer *forgiveness*. This gratuitous act attests to active cooperation with divine grace—manifesting faith, hope, and love—in their lived Christian lives.

The slaughter of those nine black women and men was motivated by festering memories of supremacy and control; it reverberated with America's original sin of racism.[42] But Roof's brutal act was met with forgiveness, love and repudiation of hate, even as family members acknowledged anger and urged his repentance and change of life. *The Washington Post* published expressions of forgiveness made by the victims' families:

> The daughter of Ethel Lance said, "I will never be able to hold her ever again, but I forgive you."
>
> Anthony Thompson, whose wife Myra died in the shooting, said, "I forgive you. My family forgives you. We would like you to take this opportunity to repent."
>
> Alana Simmons, granddaughter of Daniel Simmons said: "Although my grandfather and the other victims died at the hands of hate ... everyone's plea for your soul, is proof they lived in love and their legacies will live in love. So hate won't win."
>
> The sister of DePayne Doctor Middleton said, "I'm a work in progress and I acknowledge that I am very angry. But ... we are the family that love built. We have no room for hate, so we have to forgive."[43]

How quick we were *as a nation* to embrace their gratuitous act as *our* own! What ambiguous relief we felt! But thoughtful and serious Christians ought not to allow the nation to confuse forgiveness with justice. Nor should thoughtful and serious Christians allow this horrific event to be swallowed up and lost to common memory in the mind-

---

[42] Jim Wallis well may be the first to have used this term ("America's Original Sin," *Sojourners*, November 1987; and "Racism: America's Original Sin," *Sojourners*, July 29, 2013) https://sojo.net/articles/remembering-trayvon/racism-americas-original-sin. Theologian James Cone has given it wide and pertinent currency, see his "Theology's Great Sin: Silence in the Face of White Supremacy." *Union Seminary Quarterly Review* 55, no. 3-4 (2001): 1-14.

[43] Elahe Izadi, "The Powerful Words of Forgiveness Delivered to Dylann Roof by Victim's Relatives," https://www.washingtonpost.com/news/post-nation/wp/2015/06/19/hate-wont-win-the-powerful-words-delivered-to-dylann-roof-by-victims-relatives/

numbing surfeit of information delivered by various forms of media. Forgiveness neither disregards, nor preempts justice; neither exempts wrongdoing from punishment, nor "sacrifices justice in a foreshortened effort to move on."[44]

The act of offering forgiveness discloses what is but the conclusion of a profound existential and spiritual process, often years in the making, through which individuals or groups come to terms with and *freely respond in love and hope* to those who perpetrate grave wrongs against them. For Christian believers, the injunction of the *New Testament* rejects revenge: *"Do not resist evil. ... Love your enemies and do good to those who hate you"* (Matthew 5:38-48). In Christian terms, the ground of forgiveness is the cross of the Crucified Jewish Jesus; there we discern the wisdom and power of God made manifest. Theologically, this denotes a basic law governing the economy of salvation: God does *not* do away with evil through power, but transforms evil into good. Bernard Lonergan names this 'the Law of the Cross.'[45] The cross and death of Jesus constitute an awakening: "an enlargement of the present and a new promise for the future."[46] The crucified Jesus enfleshes *for all of us* the very meaning of being human, of being a person who embraces and lives out God's gracious gift of freedom in love and hope.

The Law of the Cross is the Law of Love: the love of an unreservedly loving God opens us *in freedom to reorient our affect*, draws us out of self-regarding self-concern, releases us from blinding bigotry, scapegoating, and hatred to find beauty and intelligence, goodness and truth in the 'other.' The love of this loving God opens us *in freedom to hope*. Hope commits us not to passive waiting, but to engaged and active trust. Even when the good is denied, frustrated, and delayed, hope strengthens our resolve to act against the radical unintelligibility of sin. Hope sustains us as we relinquish personal securities and advantage for the sake of accomplishing the human good—*together*.

---

[44] Minow, *Between Vengeance and Forgiveness*, 15.
[45] Lonergan writes: "Divine wisdom had ordained and divine goodness has willed, not to do away with the evils of the human race through power, but to convert those evils into a supreme good according to the just and mysterious Law of the Cross" (DVI, 17, art. 23).
[46] Sebastian Moore, *The Crucified Jesus Is No Stranger* (New York/ Mahwah, N.J.: Paulist Press, 1977), 75.

The Law of the Cross is the Law of Love: Love opposes revenge: It may be difficult to withhold vengeance on those who harm us, but it is *not* impossible. The families of the women and men murdered in Mother Emanuel AME Church demonstrate this clearly. It is the very nature of love to resist harming others, to transcend vengeance. And because of such transcendent love, it is possible to move beyond revenge to forgiveness, and beyond forgiveness to reconciliation.

The journey toward reconciliation is neither simple, nor easy to make; daily living by the Law of the Cross is both difficult and hard. In the context of a society or a nation, such reconciliation is even more difficult, harder. Certainly, reconciliation calls for re-education and disciplining of personal, communal, and national imagination, for envisioning something quite new even as it requires preparation for what is unexpected, without foreclosing surprise. This entails individual, communal, and national examination of conscience, concerted 'letting-go' of bigotry, hatred, and false pride. Reconciliation concretely puts hope into action: In other words, reconciliation must be embodied cognitively and affectively: For the new to come about, participation is crucial: we cannot participate as robotic entities, gathering together stubbornly or grudgingly or arrogantly. Commemoration assumes interpersonal interaction. If we are to participate fully, to engage one another appropriately, then we must retrain *affect.* We must overcome indifference and learned social obstacles to spontaneous intersubjectivity. Moreover, commemoration compels us to overcome ignorance of one another. To acquire even rudimentary knowledge of the discrete ethnic-racial, cultural groups of this nation is a large undertaking, but commemorating guides us *from* individual and group *to* common memory.

According to Edward Casey, the act of commemorating

> creates new forms of sociality, new modes of interconnection: between past and present, self and other, one group and another ... constituting a shared identity more lasting and more significant than would be possible in an uncommemorated existence. ... Rather than looking back only, commemoration concerns itself with "what, lasting, comes toward us."[47]

---

[47] Casey, *Remembering*, 251.

On a Christian account the *only* act of commemoration that lasts, the *only* act of commemoration that transcends and transvalues temporality is the Eucharistic act. Christ comes toward us with the lasting offer of his body and blood and around the table he sets *all are—all must be—*welcome.

The vicious events of centuries of slavery cannot be undone, cannot be erased. Time cannot be reversed, cannot be unraveled. The losses of slavery and the losses that slavery signifies can be neither restored nor redressed. Such losses are irreparable and, Jamaica Kincaid declares, "can be assuaged only by the impossible."[48] Eucharist *is* the impossible—not stoic forgetfulness, not romantic "glimmerings of a prelapsarian wholeness."[49] Eucharist radically challenges the *significance* time past exerts over our present and interrupts slavery's 'haunting' of that present. At the same time, Eucharist leads us to uncover and to face up to the lingering conflicts presented by slavery's past and our present. For as Saidiya Hartman reminds us, we too live in the time of slavery: By this she means, we live in the time slavery created. Eucharist draws us together in searching scrutiny of our most fundamental commitments to God and to one another.

Conclusion

I have been reflecting on the risk of memory and the cost of forgetting. Forgiveness and reconciliation are ever in our hearts, but falter on our lips, for those words as originating and grounding *can never be cheap*. In risking memory, overcoming forgetfulness, collectively taking responsibility, commemorating, we lovingly embody ethical responsibility for the past in the present for the future. The love of an unreservedly loving God will hold and support us in our risk, will not allow us to forget, and will feed us with bread and wine that lasts.

---

[48] Saidiya Hartman, "The Time of Slavery," *The South Atlantic Quarterly*, Vol. 101, No. 4 (Fall 2002): 772.

[49] Hartman, "The Time of Slavery," *The South Atlantic Quarterly*, Vol. 101, No. 4 (Fall 2002): 775.

Works Cited

Alexander, Michelle. *The New Jim Crow: Mass Incarceration in the Age of Colorblindness*. New York: The New Press, 2010.

Ainslie, Ricardo C. "Trauma, Community, and Contemporary Racial Violence: Reflections on the Architecture of Memory." 313, In *The Ethics of Remembering and the Consequences of Forgetting: Essays on Trauma, History, and Memory*, edited by Michael O'Loughlin. Lanham: Rowman & Littlefield, 2015.

Berlin, Ira. Ira Berlin, "Coming to Terms with Slavery in Twenty-First Century America." In *Slavery and Public History: The Tough Stuff of American History*, edited by James Oliver and Lois E. Horton, 1-18. Chapel Hill: University of North Carolina Press, 2006.

Blustein, Jeffrey. *The Moral Demands of Memory*. Cambridge: Cambridge University Press, 2008.

Caruth, Cathy. "Trauma and Experience." In *Theories of Memory: A Reader*, edited by Michael Rossington and Anne Whitehead, 199-205. Baltimore: The Johns Hopkins University Press, 2007.

Casey, Edward S. *Remembering: A Phenomenological Study* 2nd ed. Bloomington and Indianapolis: Indiana University Press, 2000.

Connerton, Paul. *The Spirit of Mourning*. Cambridge: Cambridge University Press, 2011.

Girard, René. *The Scapegoat,* Translated by Yvonne Freccero. Baltimore: The Johns Hopkins University Press, 1986.

Halbwachs, Maurice. *The Collective Memory*. New York: Harper-Colophon Books, 1950.

Hartman, Saidiya. "The Time of Slavery." *The South Atlantic Quarterly*, Vol. 101, No. 4 (Fall 2002): 757-777.

Kaplan, Sara. "Souls at the Crossroads, Africans on the Water: The Politics of Diasporic Melancholia." *Callaloo*, Vol. 30, No. 2 (Spring 2007): 511-526.

Kranish, Michael. "Remembrance of Crimes Past," *The Boston Sunday Globe*, July 5, 2015, A7.

Lonergan, Bernard. *Method in Theology* (New York: Herder & Herder, 1972).

Metz, Johann Baptist. *Faith in History and Society: Toward a Practical Fundamental Theology*. Translated by J. Matthew Ashley. New York: Crossroad Publishing Company, 2007.

Minow, Martha. *Between Vengeance and Forgiveness*. Boston: Beacon Press, 1998.

Moore, Sebastian. *The Crucified Jesus Is No Stranger*. New York/Mahwah, N.J.: Paulist Press, 1977.

Richter, Gerhard. "Acts of Memory and Mourning: Derrida and the Fictions of Anteriority." In *Memory, History, Theories, and Debates*, edited by Susannah Radstone and Bill Schwarz, 150-160. New York: Fordham University Press, 2010.

Ricoeur, Paul. *Memory, History, Forgetting*. Translated by Kathleen Blamey and David Pellauer. Chicago and London: University of Chicago Press, 2004.

Ruti, Mari. "Is Autonomy Unethical? Trauma and the Politics of Responsibility." 51, In *The Ethics of Remembering and the Consequences of Forgetting: Essays on Trauma, History, and Memory*, edited by Michael O'Loughlin, 37-53. Lanham: Rowman & Littlefield, 2015.

Stuntz, William J. *The Collapse of American Criminal Justice*. Cambridge, MA: The Belknap Press of Harvard University, 2011.

Volf, Miroslav. *The End of Memory*. Grand Rapids, Michigan / Cambridge, U.K.: William B. Eerdmans Publishing Company, 2006.

Theological Anthropology in the Theology of Marriage and Family[1]

Dr. Joseph S. Flipper
Bellarmine University
Louisville, Kentucky

Abstract: The Catholic Church is faced with the challenge of theologically interpreting families that have experienced divorce, remarriage, and children outside of wedlock. The anthropology of conjugal self-gift, though valuable as an analogy to the Trinitarian communion, makes the nuclear family into an ideal. Since fewer than half of children in the U.S. live in the "traditional family," it remains a problematic ideal. I suggest that familial and marital situations outside of the norm—often seen as problems illustrative of the breakdown of marriage in contemporary society—may be regarded in another light. A more adequate anthropology must consider how diverse marital and family forms can contribute to a theology of marriage.

Keywords: Anthropology, Marriage, Norm, Separation, Divorce, Traditional Family

The meaning and practice of marriage is at the heart of a contemporary Catholic crisis of identity. Because many forms of societal and political institution that bound modern people to religion have largely dissolved, the parish and the family have become the primary

---

[1] This is an expanded version of the paper I gave at "The Theological Enterprise in Light of the New Evangelization,"a Multi-Society Workshop for Theologians and Bishop sponsored by the United States Conference of Catholic Bishops on March 13, 2015, Washington D.C. Representing the Black Catholic Theological Symposium, I responded to the prompt, "What anthropology is essential to a proper understanding of marriage?" The topics addressed by the workshop are inspired by the recent extraordinary synod of Catholic bishops and the Relatio Synodi. The original version of the document was published in Italian as III Conventus Generalis Extraodinarii Episcoporum Synodi, "Relatio Synodi: Provocationes pastorales aetatis nostrae de re familiari in Evangelizationis conexu," in *Acta Apostolicae Sedis*106 no 11 (November 07, 2014), Vatican City: Libreria Editrice Vaticana, 2014, 887-908. The English translation is III Extraordinary General Assembly of the Synod of Bishops, "Relatio Synodi: Pastoral Challenges of the Family in the Context of Evangelization," *The Vatican*, last modified October 19, 2014,
http://www.vatican.va/roman_curia/synod/documents/rc_synod_doc_20141018_r elatio-synodi-familia_en.html

standing institutions of faith. Naturally, marriage, the family, and sexuality have become flashpoints over Christian identity and the authority in the Catholic Church.[2] In our contemporary context, divorce and remarriage, out-of-wedlock births, same-sex marriage, single parent homes, and cohabitation before and apart from marriage have placed additional stress on Catholic identity and challenge the intelligibility of Catholic teaching on matters of marriage and family. The recent emphasis on marriage and family in synodal and episcopal teaching reflects these challenges.[3]

Recent documents from the United States Conference of Catholic Bishops (USCCB) teaching look to human nature as a source for addressing complex pastoral issues and challenges to Christian marriage. Human nature is conceived as the universal and essential structure of human beings that can be grasped by the power of human reason. This account of human nature makes normative certain marriage and family arrangements built around the core of conjugal love and the nuclear family. There is a tension insofar as the arguments that ground marriage in an account of the human person make normative family and spousal arrangements that simply do not exist for many people. This tension is not merely a dissonance between traditional Catholic accounts of marriage and a contemporary culture that fails to appreciate it. Rather, it is a dissonance between the philosophical/theological account of human nature and the lived experience of being human. What we often imagine as exceptions to the model of normative family arrangements—divorce, divorced and remarried couples, foster parent/child relationships, childless marriages, step parent/child relationships, other mothering, and grandparents as primary caretakers—are in reality closer to the norm. They constitute the historical and existential situation of human beings, yet are not represented in accounts of human nature.

---

[2] Since *Casti connubii* (1931) and *Humanae vitae* (1968), sexual ethics and reproduction were placed at the center of this crisis. See Leslie Woodcock Tentler, "Souls and Bodies: The Birth Control Controversy and the Collapse of Confession," in Michael J. Lacey and Francis Oakley, eds., *The Crisis of Authority in Catholic Modernity* (Oxford: Oxford University Press, 2011), 293-315.

[3] The Extraordinary Synod of Catholic Bishops (2014) has taken up the challenge of addressing issues surrounding marriage and family in contemporary society. "Relatio Synodi: Pastoral Challenges of the Family in the Context of Evangelization"(2014), the final document produced by the Synod, addresses key challenges facing married couples and families. The World Meeting of Families in Philadelphia in September of 2015 recognizes the family as the natural milieu of Christian life.

In what follows, I present a brief review of the intersection of anthropology, family, and marriage in recent episcopal documents. These episcopal teachings articulate an anthropology in which the nuclear family is normative. Second, I argue that relationships often imagined as departing from normative family relationships are sufficiently common that they cannot be called exceptions. Third, I develop an outline of the traditional three ends of marriage, reconceived in light of contemporary situations and pastoral conditions. I suggest that an adequate theology of marriage must draw also from those exceptions as sources for understanding its very nature.

I. Anthropology, Marriage, and Family

The connection between anthropology and marriage is prominent in recent episcopal responses to the controversy over civil same-sex marriage. Archbishop Salvatore J. Cordileone, the chairman of the USCCB Subcommittee for the Promotion and Defense of Marriage, issued a press release responding to the Supreme Court of the United States to review a decision by the Sixth Circuit Court over marriage laws in Kentucky, Michigan, Ohio, and Tennessee. He wrote,

> It's hard to imagine how the essential meaning of marriage as between the two sexes, understood in our nation for over two hundred years, and consistent with every society throughout all of human history, could be declared illegal. To those arguing for a constitutional redefinition of marriage, one must ask: when did the Constitution suddenly mandate a novel and unfounded definition of marriage?...The central issue at stake is: what is marriage? The answer is: a bond which unites a man and a woman to each other and to any children who come from their union. Only a man and a woman can unite their bodies in a way that creates a new human being. Marriage is thus a unique and beautiful reality which a society respects to its benefit or ignores to its peril.[4]

For Cordileone, there exists a clear link between human nature and Christian marriage. The natural structure of the human being—involving a description of sexual complimentarity and the union of bodies that leads to procreation—constitutes the basis for a particular understanding

---

[4] United States Conference of Catholic Bishops, "USCCB Chairman Responds to Supreme Court Decision to Take Marriage Cases," USCCB, last modified January 16, 2015, www.usccb.org/news/2015/15-011.cfm

of marriage, as a lifelong, exclusive, public relationship open to procreation between one man and one woman. Cordileone's statement typifies recent episcopal approaches to grounding Christian marriage in an account of human nature.

In an effort to address pastoral challenges to marriage, the USCCB pastoral letter, *Marriage: Love and Life in the Divine Plan* (2009), grounds its understanding of marriage in an account of human nature and, then, examines marriage as a sacrament.[5] The bishops write, "Our pastoral letter is an invitation to discover, or perhaps rediscover, the blessing given when God first established marriage as a natural institution and when Christ restored and elevated it as a sacramental sign of salvation."[6] The document presents marriage as a relationship ordained by God that constitutes a symbolic anticipation of salvation.

The section titles of the letter reflect its method: Part I is entitled "Marriage in the Order of Creation: The Natural Institution of Marriage" and Part II is entitled "Marriage in the Order of the New Creation: The Sacrament of Matrimony." The dyad of creation/new creation parallels the dyad natural/sacramental. Part I's treatment of marriage avoids a merely philosophical or sociological treatment of marriage as a merely *natural* institution as opposed to a *supernatural* reality. Instead, it exegetes the Old Testament, especially Genesis, for an understanding of marriage in the economy of salvation.[7] The opposition between marriage as a "natural institution" and as a "sacrament" serves to show that marriage is (nearly) universal reality discovered beyond Christian society, and that God has elevated marriage to be a means of salvation.

Where *Marriage: Love and Life in the Divine Plan* treats contemporary controversies, the creation/new creation dyad effectively becomes a natural/supernatural dyad. Emphasizing the universality of human nature, the bishops explain, "marriage is also a natural blessing

---

[5] The USCCB has prioritized "strengthening marriage and family life" as the first of four Conference-wide initiatives in 2008-2012 and in 2013-2016.

[6] United States Conference of Catholic Bishops, *Marriage: Love and Life in the Divine Plan: A Pastoral Letter of the United States Conference of Catholic Bishops* (Washington D.C.: USCCB Publishing, 2009), 6, www.usccb.org/issues-and-action/marriage-and-family/marriage/love-and-life/upload/pastoral-letter-marriage-love-and-life-in-the-divine-plan.pdf. The document follows the three Augustinian goods of marriage—*bonum prolis* (offspring), *bonum fidei* (faithfulness), and *bonum sacramenti* (the indissoluble bond)—in two parts. Part I gives primary attention to procreation and union (*bonum prolis* and *bonum fidei*) while Part II treats marriage as a sacrament (*bonum sacramenti*).

[7] This exegesis is dependent upon Pope John Paul II's theology of the body and recent papal teaching.

and gift for everyone in all times and cultures."[8] Referring obliquely to same-sex marriage, the document states, "we bishops feel compelled to speak out against all attempts to redefine marriage so that it would no longer be exclusively the union of a man and a woman as God established and blessed it in the natural created order."[9] Here, "natural order" is conflated with "created order." This conflation is significant, for it implies that the concept of marriage interpreted from the book of Genesis—as a union between one man and one woman involving procreation—can be known and understood within every society on the basis of a rational examination of human nature and human society. Without this claim to universality there is no basis to claim that the nature of marriage can be known and understood by non-Christians or that a particular understanding of marriage should be enshrined in law. In a similar way, the USCCB website emphasizes emphatically that the benefits of marriage to spouses, children, and society are universal and can be understood apart from explicit religious commitment.[10]

Drawing from a range of ecclesial documents, *Marriage: Love and Life in the Divine Plan* outlines an anthropology of personal exchange as the basis of marriage. Marriage involves conjugal love, the "complete and total gift of self between husband and wife," which constitutes a communion of persons.[11] The communion of persons constituted by the marriage of a man and woman uniquely joins "life and love." Spousal unity and sexual reproduction are, it claims, the inseparable ends (or purposes or goods) of marriage. A life lived in union with the other is the first end of marriage. Quoting from *Gaudiam et Spes*, the document names the "procreation and education of offspring" as the second end. Reflecting Augustine's three goods of marriage, procreation includes the care for and raising of the child:

> "The procreative meaning of marriage involves not only the conception of children, but also their upbringing and education, including spiritual formation in the life of love. This formation can take place only within a human community formed in love. The loving communion of the

---

[8] *Marriage: Love and Life in the Divine Plan*, 4.
[9] Ibid.
[10] "To be sure, these goods are affirmed and reinforced by most religions. But they do not rely on any religious premises; they are based instead on the nature of the human person and are accessible to right reason." United States Conference of Catholic Bishops, "Marriage: Unique for a Reason," *USCCB*, www.marriageuniqueforareason.org/faq/#sec3q6
[11] *Marriage: Love and Life in the Divine Plan*, 8.

spouses is the primary context in which children are both conceived and brought up in love."[12]

Marriage: Love and Life in the Divine Plan frames the procreative and unitive ends as the inseparable elements of mutual self-gift. By implication, the dimension of interpersonal gift is lacking if one of these elements is missing. Procreation should not take place apart from unity with one's spouse, and union with one's spouse involves the procreative.

In addition, *Marriage: Love and Life in the Divine Plan* elaborates the social role of the family in reference to an anthropology of interpersonal self-gift. The familial communion forms the superstructure for the family's social role:

> With regard to the good of the children, a stable marriage between the parents is—the most human and humanizing context for welcoming children, the context which most readily provides emotional security and guarantees greater unity and continuity in the process of social integration and education. The findings of the social sciences confirm that the best environment for raising children is a stable home provided by the marriage of their parents.[13]

The pastoral document clearly implies the nuclear family as the normative social unit, the "original cell of social life."[14] The total mutual self-gift of the spouses forms the ecology for a loving and life-giving familial communion of persons. The familial communion of persons generates and sustains the communion of persons in society. The social role of the family reduces to a dynamic internal to the spousal communion.

While the pastoral letter admits social and economic challenges exist for Christian marriage, it points out several challenges that it describes as "fundamental": contraception, same-sex unions, divorce, and cohabitation. These are fundamental insofar as they challenge "the meaning and purposes" of Christian marriage itself, that is, the inseparability of the procreative and unitive meanings. It is on the basis of the anthropological account of marriage as a total self-donation—in its inseparable procreative and unitive aspects—that the document analyzes

---

[12] Ibid., 16.
[13] Ibid., 27-28. Referring to Institute for American Values, "Why Marriage Matters: Twenty-Six Conclusions from the Social Sciences," Institute for American Values, http://americanvalues.org/catalog/pdfs/why_marriage_matters2.pdf
[14] Ibid., 28. Quoting from *The Catechism of the Catholic Church* (Vatican City: Libreria Editrice Vaticana, 2000), no. 2207.

the fundamental challenges to Christian marriage. For example, arguing the benefits of marriage over cohabitation, the U.S. Bishops indicate that cohabitation represents a failure to make a complete commitment to the other. In this way, the pastoral diagnoses various failures in Christian marriage in reference to an anthropology of interpersonal self-gift.

The key problem with the anthropological approach in *Marriage* is that by making conjugal love the sole generative basis for family life, elements of marriage and family life that are not sustained by conjugal love, or are merely tangential to it, are displaced as unessential.[15] Take, for example, a married couple who are the primary caretakers for the children of a relative. Their commitment to these non-biological children is not directly implied by their complete self-gift to one another. Like foster parenting, the care for children in a single-parent household is not essentially related to an ongoing conjugal relationship. The single-parent household is diagnosed as lacking something essential, regardless of the history or concrete conditions of that household.[16] Because other forms of marriage and family organization—like foster families and step families, and practices such as othermothering, a woman caring for children not her own—are not sustained by a narrowly defined conjugal relationship, they fall outside of the norm by definition. If the family is sustained by the spousal communion of persons, it is difficult to see how non-nuclear families and extended families can be understood as authentically family.[17] By presenting conjugal love as the exclusive basis for family life, *Marriage* neglects to account for non-nuclear families.

---

[15] Similarly, David Matzko McCarthy criticizes a tendency in contemporary personalist accounts of marriage to emphasize relationships interior to the marriage and family at the expense of external relationships. McCarthy recognizes in the account of marriage as interpersonal communion congruence with what he calls the "closed family" or "self-contained home" or nuclear family, which prizes its "emotional and financial independence." David Matzko McCarthy, *Sex and Love in the Home: A Theology of the Household* (London: SCM, 2004), 93. In this model of marriage, relationships to the *outside* become optional and unessential to the happiness of domestic life. For McCarthy, the emphasis on conjugal love risks relegating social justice, relationship with community, relationship with the church to the outside of marriage itself.
[16] In contrast, *Follow the Way of Love: A Pastoral Message of the U.S. Catholic Bishops to Families On the Occasion of the United Nations 1994 International Year of the Family* (1994) largely avoids the problem of the closed nuclear family by beginning with a diversity of forms of family structure and life.
[17] There is also a danger that the anthropology of self-gift serves a nuclear family ideal that contains strong racial and class biases. See Isabel Heinemann, "Preserving the Family and the Nation: Eugenic Masculinity Concepts, Expert Intervention, and the American Family in the United States," in *Masculinities and the Nation in the Modern World: Between Hegemony and Marginalization*, ed. Pablo

Despite having the merit of holding together sexuality, reproduction, and interpersonal relationship, the anthropology of self-gift presents an incomplete foundation for understanding for marriage and family. It yields a norm—an ideal of marriage as an unreserved interpersonal union and, by extension, the family that is rooted in that union—that is insulated from the complex situations in which marriage exists. Yet these other forms of marriage and family can and do pursue authentic interpersonal and social goods, even if they do not fit neatly into a philosophical anthropology of self-gift. As a result, this anthropology may misdiagnose the challenges to Christian marriage and misdiagnose diverse family arrangements and composition as mere aberrations. Because many people experience the ideal as practically unattainable (or a too-late-to-be-attained ideal), it risks becoming a falsification and a pastoral liability. If marriage is part of God's plan for human beings and rooted in our nature, we must discover how in a variety of circumstances, we can continue to live life within that plan.

II. Anthropology and the Experience of American Catholic Families

Recent episcopal letters and individual bishops appeal to an account of human nature to make the nuclear family with a married couple and biological offspring the normative model of marriage and family life. Other arrangements fall short of this ideal. The lived realities in the United States show diverse and complex forms of family and domestic structure. A headline from a recent Pew Research Center article reads "Fewer than half of U.S. kids today live in a 'traditional' family."[18] It is true for my extended family members, who have experienced out-of-wedlock birth, cohabitation, divorce, remarriage, adoption, step-parenting, marriage without children, and othermothering. Recent studies from the Pew Research Center, The Center for Applied Research in the Apostolate, the National Survey of Family Growth, and the General Social Survey confirm that many American families look like mine.[19]

Dominguez Andersen and Simon Wendt (New York: Palgrave Macmillan, 2015), 71-92.

[18] Gretchen Livingston, "Fewer than half of U.S. kids today live in a 'traditional' family," *Pew Research Center*, last modified December 22, 2014, www.pewresearch.org/fact-tank/2014/12/22/less-than-half-of-u-s-kids-today-live-in-a-traditional-family/

[19] I admit my interpretation of the realities affecting marriage and family life drawn here is incomplete. I have sought to provide an accurate picture of the facts from

A significant percentage of Catholics are divorced, separated, or living with a partner. According to the 2015 Pew U.S. Religious Landscape Survey, 8% of Catholics are living with a partner, 12% of Catholics are currently divorced or separated, 7% are widowed, 21% have never married, and 52% of Catholics are currently married.[20] The 2007 Center for Applied Research in the Apostolate (CARA) study finds that 4% of Catholics are living with a partner, 1% of Catholics are separated, and 12% divorced, while 53% are married.[21] The same survey finds that 11% of Catholics who are currently married have been divorced. The General Social Survey 2014 data indicate that 32% of Catholics who have been married divorced at some point in their life.[22] In sum, more than one in ten American Catholics are currently divorced and not remarried and almost one in three Catholics who have been married have divorced at some point in their life.

The statistics on childbirth indicate that most first children are born to unmarried parents. The National Survey of Family Growth (NFSG) indicates that in 2011-2013 48.3% of mothers 15-44 years of age were married when their first child was born.[23] 28.6% were cohabiting while 25.2% were unmarried and not cohabitating. While 57% of fathers 15-44 years of age were currently or formerly married to the child's mother at the time of their first child's birth, a full 26.4% were cohabitating and

---

the following social scientific sources: Pew Research Center, "America's Changing Religious Landscape," (May 12, 2015); Mark M. Gray, Paul M. Perl, and Tricia C. Bruce, "Marriage in the Catholic Church: A Survey of U.S. Catholics," Center for Applied Research in the Apostolate (October 2007); National Survey of Family Growth, "Key Statistics from the National Survey of Family Growth-B Listing," *National Center for Health Statistics*, last modified April 20, 2015, http://www.cdc.gov/nchs/nsfg/key_statistics/b.htm; and Tom W. Smith, Peter V. Marsden, and Michael Hout, "General Social Survey, 1972-2010," Cumulative File ICPSR31521-v1 (Chicago, IL: National Opinion Research Center, distributed by Ann Arbor, MI: Inter-university Consortium for Political and Social Research, 2011).
[20] Pew Research Center, "America's Changing Religious Landscape," (May 12, 2015), 62.
[21] Mark M. Gray, Paul M. Perl, and Tricia C. Bruce, "Marriage in the Catholic Church: A Survey of U.S. Catholics," Center for Applied Research in the Apostolate (October 2007), 18.
[22] Tom W. Smith, Peter V. Marsden, and Michael Hout, "General Social Survey, 1972-2010," Cumulative File ICPSR31521-v1 (Chicago, IL: National Opinion Research Center, distributed by Ann Arbor, MI: Inter-university Consortium for Political and Social Research, 2011).
[23] National Survey of Family Growth, "Key Statistics from the National Survey of Family Growth-B Listing," *National Center for Health Statistics*, last modified April 20, 2015, http://www.cdc.gov/nchs/nsfg/key_statistics/b.htm, Based on Gladys Martinez, Kimberly Daniels, and Anjani Chandra, Division of Vital Statistics "Fertility of Men and Women Aged 15–44 Years in the United States: National Survey of Family Growth, 2006–2010," *National Health Statistics Reports*, 51 (April 12, 2012), 19.

16.4% were unmarried and not cohabitating.[24] Of all the first-born children in the United States, over half have parents that are not married at the time of the child's birth.

Almost ten percent of children live with non-biological parents, not including arrangements such as living with grandparents. According to 2010 U.S. Census data, 92.3% of all children of householders are biological children, 2.5% are adopted, and 5.2% are stepchildren. In the 12-14 age range, 2.7% are adopted and 6.4% are stepchildren. In the 15-18 age range, 2.7% are adopted and 7.1% are stepchildren.[25] The NSFG indicates that 11.3% of women 18-44 years of age have cared for a non-biological child in 2011-2013. This statistic does not account for grandparents 45 years or older as primary caretakers. While most children are living with biological parents, around 8% of all children are adopted or stepchildren, and the percentage of adopted or stepchildren increases with the age of the children. With over one in ten women caring for a non-biological child, family composition often reflects arrangements other than the nuclear family.

Though this survey of the data is incomplete, it provides a window into the lived realities of many American Catholics that theologians and pastors must honestly address.[26] The prevalence of divorce, high out-of-wedlock childbirth rates, and a variety of family structures present a radical disjunction between the image of marriage presented by a philosophical anthropology and the lived reality of marriage and family life. The closed, nuclear family presents a problematic ideal.[27] While grounding marriage in conjugal love does affirm a connection between marriage and procreation, it does not account for the variety of marriage and family arrangements.

The data suggest the need to reconsider the role of theological anthropology in developing a theology of marriage. The anthropology of

---

[24] Ibid.
[25] Rose M. Kreider and Daphne A. Lofquist, "Adopted Children and Stepchildren: 2010: Population Characteristics," U.S. Census Bureau (April 2014), 4.
[26] Similarly, Peter Steinfels recently called for honestly addressing the disjunction between the teaching on contraception of *Humanae vitae* and the lived experience of lay Catholics. Peter Steinfels, "Contraception and Honesty: A Proposal for the Next Synod," *Commonweal* 142, no 10 (May 14, 2015): 12-19.
[27] Contemporary challenges to marriage may indicate the demise of the *closed* nuclear family, but may not mean the demise of the family itself. Lisa Sowle Cahill argues the nuclear family is really a modern construction and that the extended family/kinship model of family is more natural to a biblical and Christian conception of family. See Lisa Sowle Cahill, *Family: A Christian Social Perspective* (Minneapolis: Fortress, 2000).

self-gift is a helpful analogy for relating human relationships and the Trinitarian communion. At the same time, making conjugal self-giving normative and foundational for family and social life obscures the other forms of loving communion present in, and often flourishing, in non-nuclear families. An account of the anthropological foundations is indispensable as long as it remains attentive to human beings in their concrete, historical situations. When we ask "what kind of anthropology is essential to a proper understanding of marriage?", *our understanding of what humanity is has to come not just from an abstract essentialist account of human nature but from concrete human beings and their real situations.* Spouses in prison, living across borders, living in poverty, working sixteen hour days, and being a foster parent or stepparent is *closer to the norm than the exception.* A proper understanding of marriage must account for how marriage functions within an economy of life and death, as a vehicle for survival, and not infrequently as an impediment to survival of the family. An adequate anthropology must account for the diversity of ways in which family life is lived.

III. The Goods of Marriage Revisited

Augustine's elaboration of the threefold good of marriage—offspring (*bonum prolis*), faithfulness (*bonum fidei*), and the marriage bond (*bonum sacramenti*)—has become a classic in Christian theology of marriage. Deriving from Augustine, there is a long tradition embedded in catechesis, preaching, and seminary instruction of speaking of the three goods or threefold of marriage. The goods of marriage relate human experience to the supernatural gift of grace. Distinguishing the three goods—the physical, psychological, and spiritual—served to correlate marriage with theological anthropology, namely the distinct human ends. Human beings possess distinct ends and operate on distinct though interrelated levels: life, the good life, and eternal life.[28] The first is the vital or biological end, namely life. The second concerns the life of virtue in community: the good life. Finally, human beings are created for union with God, eternal life. While we can distinguish between these various levels, each is connected in human experience: friendship and

---

[28] I am grateful to M. Shawn Copeland of Boston College for her perspectives on the threefold end from Bernard Lonergan. Lonergan relates the threefold good of marriage to a threefold and hierarchical human end: life, the good life, and eternal life. See Bernard J. F. Lonergan, "Finality, Love, and Marriage," in *Collection*, ed. Frederick E. Crowe and Robert M. Doran, Collected Works of Bernard Lonergan 4 (Toronto: University of Toronto, 1988), 17-52.

grace are not disconnected from the vital level. A meal shared (vital level) can be the opportunity for friendship (virtue), and occasion the communion with God in the Eucharist (grace). Marriage may be interpreted according to these ends: On the vital level, marriage has *life* as its end. On the level of virtue, marriage is a friendship between the partners. On the level of eternal life, marriage conduces to the sanctification of the married partners. In marriage, the cooperation in providing concrete necessities for each other and for children becomes the opportunity for friendship, and the occasion for grace. What follows is a reflection on the classic goods of marriage in light of the realities of marriage and family in contemporary life.

a. The Vital Level: Survival

Marriage serves not only procreation of offspring, but also survival, which requires networks of support outside the nuclear family. I am married and we are blessed with children. In my everyday experience, being married primarily concerns the practical realities of life—being together, cleaning up, and taking care of tasks. Keeping children clean, clothed, and socialized to the world are exhausting tasks, even for a husband and wife who are employed and able-bodied. I am aware that my wife and I are interdependent to provide stability and to supply basic needs to our children. However, these needs cannot be fully satisfied within the nuclear family, since we are dependent upon others to educate our children and sometimes care for them. My church is a small parish in Louisville, Kentucky. Many members of the community are immigrants, non-native English speakers, and almost everyone has family living across borders. For my family, but also for many in our church, the mutual cooperation and mutual dependence entailed by marriage serves the purpose of survival.

Many survive without a spouse present, whether due to migration, separation, divorce, or death. For many people, especially women, marriage has often been an insecure proposition. In some communities, people have not always been afforded the opportunity to marry. Historically, American slavery meant that a woman's body was property destined for breeding and that her husband and children could be sold away. The punishment and incarceration of black men under Jim Crow systematically placed black fathers at risk. Today, the prison- and detention-industrial complex functions to incarcerate a significant percentage of black and Latino fathers. Due to systems that prevent spouses from being together or that dis-incentivize marriage, many women have generated ways of "surviving and flourishing" apart from marriage and apart from spouses living under the same roof, including practices of "othermothering" and "community mothering."[29] The classic good of marriage—procreation—should be understood within the broader familial task of survival, common to spouses without children, to single parents, and to nuclear families.

The vital good of marriage, therefore, is shared by many forms of family structure that are necessary for survival. This understanding is consonant with Pope John Paul II's theology of the body in which the body carries a theological meaning and is the entry point for friendship and grace. In the words of Pope John Paul II, "the body through its own visibility manifests [the person] and, manifesting [the person], acts as intermediary, that is, enables man and woman, right from the beginning, 'to communicate' with each other according to that *communion personarum* [communion of persons] willed by the Creator precisely for them."[30] Similarly, M. Shawn Copeland presents the body as the image of God and the locus of communion. Against the dehumanization of slavery and racism, black women reclaimed a freedom of the flesh and embodied solidarity.[31] God's image is engrained in the flesh. Communion with others and with God is possible only by being a body. The practices of survival that mediate human flourishing and communion with others can be found in diversely constituted families and marriages.

b. The Level of Virtue: The Good Life

On the level of virtue, the human goal is not just life, but the "good life." Human beings are fulfilled by a life of virtue lived in community and friendship. Contemporary theological treatments of marriage—

---

[29] Karen Teel, *Racism and the Image of God* (New York: Palgrave Macmillan, 2010), 95.
[30] John Paul II, "General Audience: The Fullness of Interpersonal Communication," (Wednesday, December 19, 1979), Vatican, https://w2.vatican.va/content/john-paul-ii/en/audiences/1979/documents/hf_jp-ii_aud_19791219.html
[31] Copeland appeals to Toni Morrison's *Beloved*, in which Baby Suggs enjoins her audience of former slaves to love their flesh: "Here, in this place, we flesh, flesh that weeps, laughs; flesh that dances on bare feet in grass. You do not love our flesh...and you do not love our neck unnoosed and straight. We got to love it! This is flesh I'm talking about here. Flesh that needs to be loved." In M. Shawn Copeland, *Enfleshing Freedom: Body, Race, and Being* (Minneapolis: Fortress, 2010), 52.

without abandoning theme of procreation and care for children—have turned to the notion of interpersonal fulfillment: friendship, life partnership, interpersonal love. Marriage fulfills part of this need for human friendship and sharing. It would be a mistake, however, to restrict the interpersonal good of marriage to the self-gift between spouses, or to restrict this good to the bounds of the home. There is a societal dimension whereby marriage orders spouses in virtuous relationship to one another and to a broader community. Marriage orients the human being to virtue because it can orient the human being to shared goods.

I experience marriage as an orientation of our lives to my spouse, to our children, and to our communities. Having young children has been an isolating experience, but it is also a grounding experience. I am now grounded to place and patterns, responsible for a small piece of earth. I am now bound to the world in a way that I wasn't prior to the birth of my first child. Marriage is creative of a relationship to a neighborhood, a church, and a public school that I didn't have before. Yet, I must recognize that the virtuous patterns of life are not only constituted in marriages like mine, but may be constituted through different kinds of family arrangements and friendships.

c. The Level of Grace: Eternal Life

Because Saint Paul believed that Jesus's return was imminent, he had a preference for celibacy and thought marriage to be a concession to human weakness. Yet, he sets both celibacy and marriage against the backdrop of the coming Kingdom, as a form of life "assigned" by the Lord (1 Cor. 7:17). The famous Pauline instruction on spousal love in Ephesians makes a parallel between the love between spouses and the love of Christ for the church. Talking about the spouses as "one flesh," Paul writes, "This is a great mystery, and I am applying it to Christ and the church" (Eph. 5:32). For Paul, *mysterion* has a broader meaning: it refers to the hidden plan of God that is unfolding through time, the mystery of the unity of the church and Christ. His instruction, evidently *directed toward real married disciples*, suggests that their spousal love participates in the unfolding of this mystery through time. The "one flesh" of the married couple is a form of life through which discipleship is lived and holiness attained. Spousal love anticipates the union of Christ with the church. Building on this Pauline perspective, the church fathers envisioned human nature as *a single, unitary* reality that had been divided by sin. Salvation was humanity united by and gathered into Christ. Marriage images and anticipates the future union of humanity through Christ.

The Pauline perspective on marriage should be applied to the diverse forms of family life.

If there is a gradualism whereby the imperfect anticipates and tends toward the perfect, it isn't that imperfect marital and family situations anticipate the perfect, autonomous nuclear family. Instead, marriage, celibacy, and diverse forms of family may anticipate the perfect union of Christ and the church.

IV. Conclusion

The Catholic Church is faced with the challenge of theologically interpreting families that have experienced divorce, remarriage, and children outside of wedlock. The anthropology of conjugal self-gift, though valuable as an analogy to the Trinitarian communion, makes the nuclear family into an ideal. Since fewer than half of children in the U.S. live in the "traditional family," it remains a problematic ideal. I suggest that familial and marital situations outside of the norm—often seen as problems illustrative of the breakdown of marriage in contemporary society—may be regarded in another light. A more adequate anthropology must consider how diverse marital and family forms can contribute to a theology of marriage.

Works Cited

Cahill, Lisa Sowle. *Family: A Christian Social Perspective*. Minneapolis: Fortress, 2000.

Copeland, M. Shawn. *Enfleshing Freedom*: *Body, Race, and Being*. Minneapolis: Fortress, 2010.

The Catechism of the Catholic Church. Vatican City: Libreria Editrice Vaticana, 2000.

Gray, Mark M., Paul M. Perl, and Tricia C. Bruce. "Marriage in the Catholic Church: A Survey of U.S. Catholics." Center for Applied Research in the Apostolate. October 2007.

Heinemann, Isabel. "Preserving the Family and the Nation: Eugenic Masculinity Concepts, Expert Intervention, and the American Family in the United States," in *Masculinities and the Nation in the Modern World: Between Hegemony and Marginalization*, edited by Pablo Dominguez Andersen and Simon Wendt, 71-92. New York: Palgrave Macmillan, 2015.

Kreider, Rose M. and Daphne A. Lofquist. "Adopted Children and Stepchildren: 2010: Population Characteristics." U.S. Census Bureau. April 2014.

Livingston, Gretchen. "Fewer than half of U.S. kids today live in a 'traditional' family." *Pew Research Center*. Last modified December 22, 2014. www.pewresearch.org/fact-tank/2014/12/22/less-than-half-of-u-s-kids-today-live-in-a-traditional-family/

Lonergan, Bernard J. F. "Finality, Love, and Marriage." In *Collection*, edited by Frederick E. Crowe and Robert M. Doran, 17-52. Collected Works of Bernard Lonergan 4. Toronto: University of Toronto, 1988.

McCarthy, David Matzko. *Sex and Love in the Home: A Theology of the Household.* London: SCM, 2004.

National Survey of Family Growth, "Key Statistics from the National Survey of Family Growth-B Listing," *National Center for Health Statistics*. Last modified April 20, 2015. http://www.cdc.gov/nchs/nsfg/key_statistics/b.htm. Based on Martinez, Gladys, Kimberly Daniels, and Anjani Chandra, Division of Vital Statistics "Fertility of Men and Women Aged 15–44 Years in the United States: National Survey of Family Growth, 2006–2010." *National Health Statistics Reports*, 51 (April 12, 2012), 19.

Pew Research Center, "America's Changing Religious Landscape." May 12, 2015.

Smith, Tom W., Peter V. Marsden, and Michael Hout. "General Social Survey, 1972-2010." Cumulative File ICPSR31521-v1. Chicago, IL: National Opinion Research Center, distributed by Ann Arbor, MI: Inter-University Consortium for Political and Social Research, 2011.

Steinfels, Peter. "Contraception and Honesty: A Proposal for the Next Synod." *Commonweal* 142, no 10 (May 14, 2015): 12-19.

Teel, Karen. *Racism and the Image of God*. New York: Palgrave Macmillan, 2010.

Tentler, Leslie Woodcock. "Souls and Bodies: The Birth Control Controversy and the Collapse of Confession." In Michael J. Lacey and Francis Oakley, eds., *The Crisis of Authority in Catholic Modernity*. Oxford: Oxford University Press, 2011. 293-315

III Conventus Generalis Extraodinarii Episcoporum Synodi. "Relatio Synodi: Provocationes pastorales aetatis nostrae de re familiari in Evangelizationis conexu." In *Acta Apostolicae Sedis* 106, no. 11 (November 07, 2014). Vatican City: Libreria Editrice Vaticana, 2014. 887-908. III Extraordinary General Assembly of the Synod of Bishops, "Relatio Synodi: Pastoral Challenges of the Family in the Context of Evangelization," *The Vatican*, last modified October 19, 2014.
http://www.vatican.va/roman_curia/synod/documents/rc_synod_d oc_20141018_relatio-synodi-familia_en.html

United States Conference of Catholic Bishops. *Marriage: Love and Life in the Divine Plan: A Pastoral Letter of the United States Conference of Catholic Bishops*. Washington D.C.: USCCB, 2009.

_____. *Follow the Way of Love: A Pastoral Message of the U.S. Catholic Bishops to Families On the Occasion of the United Nations 1994 International Year of the Family*. Washington D.C.: USCCB, 1994.

_____. "USCCB Chairman Responds to Supreme Court Decision to Take Marriage Cases." *USCCB*. Last modified January 16, 2015. www.usccb.org/news/2015/15-011.cfm

Book Reviews

Black Practical Theology, edited by Dale P. Andrews and Robert London Smith Jr. x, 350 pp. Baylor University Press, Waco TX, 2015. $49.95 (paperback). ISBN-13:9781602584358

Dale P. Andrews and Robert London Smith, edited collection of essays in *Black Practical Theology* represents a significant contribution to the discourse on Practical Theology. The discipline of practical theology primarily addresses critical thinking about what we do and how we live out faith. As stated in an earlier book, *Invitation to Practical Theology: Catholic Voices and Visions (Paulist Press, 2014)*, includes the study of practices, contexts, cultures and communities in dialogue with faith traditions and informed by human knowledge.

Dale P. Andrews has been a prominent black voice in this discourse with his previous book, *Practical Theology for Black Churches: Bridging Black Theology and African American Folk Religion.* (Westminster John Knox Press, 2002). In that book, Andrews helped to define practical theology in a way that the black minister or scholar could better understand and appreciate. He saw that there was a chasm between the academy of black theology and black churches. This widening chasm critiqued the role and purpose of black theologians in the life of the black community. His hope in his earlier book was to "bridge the theological axioms of black theology and the faith claims operating in African American folk religion. He was able in the earlier book to make palpable the idea of black theology's contribution to black life. The missing piece in the earlier book, was the voice of black pastoral leaders. This omission has been rectified in this new collection of essays. The purpose of this new contribution to the discourse on practical theology is to "bring into dialogue with church and parachurch leaders in the black communities select scholars who are working within the constructive, biblical and ethics disciplines of black theology and those scholars who work within practical theology and its customary subdisciplines. The hope for Andrews and Smith, is to create a "trialogue" between these various communities. These three dialogue partners are 1) scholars from among the traditional subdisciplines of practical theology (homiletics, Christian education, pastoral care and counseling); 2) dialogue partners from either constructive, biblical or ethics theological disciplines and 3) finally the third partner chosen was a prominent black church pastor or parachurch leader who exhibited significant ministerial presence in the black community. The areas that they address include Black Youth, Education/Class and Poverty; Gender, Sexual Orientation and Race; Globalism, Immigration and Diasporan communities; Health Care and HIV/AIDS; Mass Incarceration and the Justice System. Contributors include well known and recognized scholars and ministers such as Diana Hayes, Phillis Sheppard and Jeremiah Wright as well as new voices in the field and landscape such as Raphael Warnock, Madipoane Masenya and Edward Antonio. The final section is written by Andrews and Smith who offer a synthesis of the text and share their own conclusions to this discourse.

Did they succeed in providing something new as well as contributing a voice(s) that has been missing from the discourse? The answer is a guarded yes. In the academy, the voices of black scholars continue to be muted or nonexistent in certain disciplines. Practical theology is one discipline that has until recently omitted the diversity of voices within the community. The editors are to be congratulated for the inclusion of essays from scholars in the Caribbean and South Africa, as well as attentiveness to an ecumenical vision (Catholic and Protestant authors. While this book is an excellent resource for students studying theology, one glaring omission in this collection of essays is the field of spiritual formation (a subdiscipline of practical theology) and liturgical studies. Hopefully revised editions of this text will include these disciplines as well as those black voices who are emerging in the "Black and Urban Education Matters" movements. As a final note, recommended companion to this book for black Catholic readers is Invitation to *Practical Theology: Catholic Voices* (Paulist Press, 2014) which includes an essay by M. Shawn Copeland, "Weaving Memory, Sturcturing Ritual, Evoking Mythos: Commemoration of the Ancestors."

Dr. C. Vanessa White
Catholic Theological Union
Chicago, Illinois

Stand Your Ground: Black Bodies and the Justice of God. Kelly Brown Douglas. Maryknoll, New York: Orbis Books, 2015. 234pp. $24.00. Paper. ISBN: 9781626981096.

Trayvon Martin and Sybrina Fulton are the immediate inspirations for *Stand Your Ground: Black Bodies and the Justice of God* by Kelly Brown Douglas. For Douglas, the mother of an African American young man, Trayvon's death and the acquittal of his killer compelled her to investigate the prevailing "Stand Your Ground" culture that condones the treatment of black bodies as little more than disposable commodities. A womanist theologian and pastor, Douglas connects the anxieties of Black mothers who are particularly afflicted by "Stand Your Ground" politics with Fulton's faithful advocacy for the full humanity of her deceased son and the enduring meaning of Trayvon's life in light of her God who is immanently just.

Douglas' intent in this work is to engage readers, as she was engaged, in philosophical, political, spiritual and maternal soul-searching on "Stand Your Ground" law and its implications for black bodies and those who trust in the justice of God. The result is a work that testifies to the power of the human story to shape across generations a people's values, principles and beliefs. In *Stand Your Ground*, the reader participates in a historical and theological exploration of the major strands of two grand narratives that undergird U.S. culture and contemporary way of life. Part One of the text chronicles the development of "American Exceptionalism", an ideology that privileges Anglo-Saxon heritage; Part Two gives an account of Black Faith, rooted in African religious traditions and shaped by the life experiences of African Americans. In competing voices, the stories speak to the nation's ongoing struggle for racial justice, evidenced most powerfully by the more recent shootings of other unarmed Black youth - Jordan Davis, Jonathan Ferrell, Renisha McBride, and Michael Brown, perhaps the most widely recognized – and the Mother Emmanuel Nine, whose execution occurred during the reviewer's reading of this text.

Douglas situates Trayvon's 21st century confrontation with "Stand Your Ground" rationale in first century German history, English common law and the philosophy of the nation's founding fathers. With thorough research, she reconstructs the case for the Anglo-Saxon myth of "American Exceptionalism", pulling back the curtain to expose cultivated ideologies that systematically promote the "hypervaluation of whiteness and the denigration of blackness (xiv)." Through the ages, America's exceptional identity, represented in Anglo-Saxon culture and language, government institutions and politics, its unique calling among nations and singular relationship with God, is rooted in the cherished purity of its Anglo-Saxon citizens. Douglas suggests that science, religion, and the law were systematically manipulated to legitimize the superiority of the white American race and accord it with extraordinary property rights that led to the extermination of Native Americans and the enslavement of Africans in the United States.

She contends that in the context of white culture ingrained in Anglo-Saxon exceptionalism, blackness is an offense to white America, blackness is a sin against God. Historically and even until today, the black body is considered "guilty chattel", a threat to "cherished white property" by virtue of its perceived hypersexuality and violent disposition. Douglas explains the problematic in terms of traditional natural law and theo-ideology that describe blackness as dangerous, criminal and surely always guilty of something. In sad summary, this is the myth and these are the grounds on which chattel slavery, the black codes, Jim Crow, lynchings, the war on drugs, the industrial prison complex and "Stand Your Ground" laws have prevailed and continue to perpetrate racialized violence against black bodies in defense of white freedoms. In her insights up to this point, Douglas provides informed affirmation, appropriate vocabulary and historic perspective to corroborate the suspicions of African Americans that the United States is protected space, a home for white supremacy.

Despite the grief and sorrow so often triggered by "Stand Your Ground" culture, Sybrina Fulton and Kelly Brown Douglas uphold another great American narrative. In Part Two, the author juxtaposes the God portrayed in the myth of American exceptionalism with the God of black faith. Although both divine personalities can be located in Sacred Scripture, in the respective prayers and religion of God's people, Douglas lifts up the story and song of God's beloved black faithful, counter-narratives to the deification of white oppression that condemns black bodies as "guilty chattel". Drawing on traditional African understandings of the Supreme Being, the author reflects on the God-given freedom and power of black believers to theologically resist the absurdity of Anglo-Saxon exceptionalism, even as they were (and remain) caught in its racist web. Here it seemed that the author missed an opportunity to more fully flesh out the African heritage of Black

Americans given the extensive research done on the construction of Anglo-Saxon identity.

However, her location of Trayvon on the cross, crucified like Jesus Christ by the same sin of a "Stand Your Ground" culture and raised to new life by the justice of God, is a poignant image that resounds with the familiar prophetic voices of faith whose truth telling in this kairos time calls humanity to renew this culture following the example of Trayvon's mother, whose hope lies in a God who is mysterious, free, just and right on time.

    Kathleen Dorsey Bellow, D.Min.
    Xavier University of Louisiana
    New Orleans, Louisiana

Democracy in Black. How Race Still Enslaves the American Soul by Eddie S. Glaude Jr. Crown Publishers, $26.00, 275 pp.

Glaude is outraged by the police killings of black people like Michael Brown, Tamir Rice, Freddy Gray, and Eric Garner, and he is inspired by the activists of the "Black Lives Matter" movement. While he teaches at Princeton, he is speaking here mainly to his black sisters and brothers. No more business as usual! In this moment in our tortured history of racial oppression, we must generate dramatic new ways of grappling with white supremacy. Glaude's other readers, also outraged by those killings, can learn here the full sweep of the crisis that now engulfs Black America and what might be done about it.

His first seven chapters describe the symptoms of the enslavement and the last two propose some transformative strategies. Not only could these bring about genuine democracy, as opposed to the sham version we have now, but they could also be the innovative steps needed to put white supremacy on the path to extinction. Yet, he admits, these strategies might well fail. If so, then US democracy will be effectively dead and the evils perpetrated by white supremacy will go on.

We really do not have genuine democracy, he argues, though most Americans like to think so. The US is effectively "Two Nations: Black and White, Separate, Hostile, Unequal," as Andrew Hacker puts it. African-Americans have always been deliberately excluded from full participation in the "American dream." Racial oppression is not some accidental aberration or occasional failure to live up to the ideals in the Declaration of Independence and the Constitution's Preamble. Rather, white supremacy is systemic, codified, and "normal." It operates in and through our political, economic, and cultural processes (which Glaude calls "racial habits") to damage and destroy black lives.

The National Urban League's 39th annual State of Black America (2015) contains the latest evidence of its workings. Research summarized in the report details the effects of racism in nearly every major "quality of life" category. As usual, the black unemployment rate is double that of whites and far worse in some metropolitan areas. For every dollar of median white household wealth, the median black household has only six cents. Over a quarter of the black population lives below the poverty line, but only 11.1% of whites do. Studies of black health care, infant mortality, and homicide rates expose the devastation of black life at the hands of white supremacy. The Urban League's CEO, Marc Morial, had it right: "I must use the word 'crisis' for the state of black America in 2015."

For Glaude, white supremacy is ultimately rooted in what he calls the "value gap," the pervasive sense that white skin designates superiority of character or culture or some mix of these, while black skin designates inferiority. This gap is taught and reinforced in the racial habits, the ways by which the systems, structures, and routines that govern daily life all convey the message: "White skinned people are inherently worth more than black skinned people."

The "business as usual" of black liberal politics does not address this value gap. It even marginalizes the realities of black suffering. For Glaude, leaders like Jesse Jackson, Al Sharpton, and, yes, even Barack Obama, have demonstrated their strategic and moral bankruptcy. Black diversity means there can no longer be one dominant black leader like King. This moment calls for creative, dramatic, and genuinely democratic initiatives at the grassroots to bring about the necessary transformation of our country.

He calls for vigorous street protests to interrupt our settled routines and compel attention to racial injustice, though he admits that their staying power is doubtful. He urges activists to form organizations focused on local issues of racial justice. When these organizations form regional and national networks of collaboration, they will revitalize democracy such that politicians can no longer ignore black suffering. Yet this strategy's effectiveness is doubtful, too. Movement and organizational leaders can drop out or be co-opted. Black people are not more virtuous and moral than other people. Failure is a real possibility.

He urges blacks to vote in the November 2016 elections, but to leave the space for President blank or simply write in "none of the above." This "blank-out campaign" will demonstrate that black voters are no longer "captured and silent." It entails huge risks to black lives and the common good, but he dismisses the risks too easily because he wants nothing less than to "remake American democracy."

Glaude envisions no significant role for white allies here, but that is not why the protests, networks, and blank-out campaign are not enough to end racial inequality. Ultimately, that requires "ridding ourselves of the value gap." This deep root of white supremacy underlies the racial habits, while the racial habits reinforce the gap. We must change those habits "that reproduce so much evil," but how can real change take place when, as he admits, the value gap will predetermine the final results every time?

He suggests the answer in his book's subtitle. Since race enslaves the soul, our very *souls* must be liberated. The value gap is more than a political and moral issue. It is fundamentally a religious challenge. "Social sin" is Catholic social teaching's term for the racial habits that reinforce the gap, but the systemic devaluation of people with black skin is actually idolatry, as James Baldwin clearly perceived. Thus, only a faith like Martin Luther King Jr's, mated with genuine and ongoing conversion, offers any hope of transforming those habits.

Nonetheless, Glaude makes an important contribution to the national soul-searching that we need so urgently. His accounts of the state of our union and the brutalities incessantly inflicted on Black America overwhelmingly support his main thesis: it is time – it is long past time! – for creative, dramatic, and democratic strategies to dismantle white supremacy. Those strategies, however, must come from a depth that Glaude acknowledges, but does not explore here.

Dr. Jon Nilson
Professor Emeritus of Theology
Loyola University Chicago
Chicago, Illinois

Book Reviews

Morality Truly Christian Truly African Foundational, Methodological, and Theological Considerations. Paulinus Ikechukwu Odozor, C.S.Sp. Notre Dame, Indiana: University of Notre Dame Press, 2014. 371pp. $40.00. Paper. ISBN: 0268037388

Father Paulinus Ikechukwu Odozor, C.S.Sp. offers extraordinary scholarship in his latest book. His bold aim is concisely stated: articulate a "Christian ethical discourse that is at once Christian and African (4)." He achieves that complex and breathtaking task beautifully. *Morality Truly Christian Truly African* will endure as an African Catholic theological ethic.

Few scholars create such a respectful and insightful conversation across diverse ecclesial, theological, cultural and academic divides. This book practices the wisdom of Vatican II in the way it exemplifies critical and charitable dialogue between tradition and culture in the "ongoing encounters and contacts" between Africans and Europeans over 500 years, in the encounter of African Traditional Religion and Christianity and its missionary impulse, and between diverse "new" theologies (Black, Womanist, Latino/a, etc.) and traditional Roman Catholic theologies (Augustine, Ambrose, Thomas Aquinas, etc.).

Odozor celebrates the fact that the "third church is here," in how most Catholics live in Latin America and the Catholic Church in Africa is growing at annual rate of over 3 percent per year with the largest seminaries in the Christian world. He articulates a richly contextualized African Catholic moral theology.

I raise two interrelated fundamental theological and ethical themes. Odozor raises complex questions of globalization and global crises afflicting the world including but not limited to "ongoing ferment" in the Catholic Church over issues of sexual ethics, ordination of women, and dissent from authoritative teachings as well as conflicts within Islam and the incapacity of the "Western liberal tradition" to justify its answers on "key issues concerning the life and destiny of the human person (65)." Simultaneously, African traditions "are struggling to survive, adjust, or renew themselves in the face of so much change, so much disequilibrium, and so much flux (65)." He underscores the frailty of humanity at this critical moment of history.

Yet I wonder if these historical and contemporary crises might be more fully engaged in both substantive and methodological ways. A classic theme in Roman Catholic theology and spirituality is that of "dark night" or "impasse," perhaps most famously articulated by Saint John of the Cross. Many theologians are engaging the theme of impasse as a fundamental category and way of contending with the multiple threats to the most basic conditions for the possibility of sustaining both human and non-human life on the planet. Engaging impasse is a way to discern the need for, and nurture openness to, the purification to which God calls people of faith and also to discern the emergence of a new way of being to which the Spirit draws humanity.

Odozor recognizes that current cultural and economic threats to an authentic humanity are no less evident in Africa. He contends that the "theologian of inculturation must have a deep knowledge of the culture in which he or she is working—that is, a deep appreciation for its strengths and honesty about its weaknesses (169)." Odozor does this well. I found joy his telling both of African religious and cultural stories and Gospel parables.

However, the substantive question of the theme of impasse also raises a methodological question. While the methodology is certainly dialogical it is not necessarily mutually correlative. It is not clear that a mutually critical interpretation of both texts and situation is operative here. Put another way, it seems that, Odozor's interpretation of a Vatican II Roman Catholic moral theology has all the answers to the crises of our time and no need for transformation itself.

I wonder if a mutually critical methodology might lead not only to deep spiritual practices of purification and openness to an unknown future led by the Spirit, it may also lead to a uniquely African Christian Catholic moral theology that exemplifies "a collaborative venture, a critical enterprise, and a discipline with big ears" that is "attuned to the movement of ideas within all parts of the world-wide Church and the global community (298)." Nevertheless, *Morality Truly Christian Truly African* stands on its own as an authoritative and enduring contribution to Roman Catholic moral theology in a global context.

Dr. Alex Mikulich
Loyola University
New Orleans, Louisiana

Racism and the Image of God. Karen Teel. New York: Palgrave Macmillan, 2010. Viii, 216 pp. $100.00. Hardcover. ISBN: 9780230622777.

A theologian serves as a midwife of God's grace to the community of believers and also as a conduit for the response of the community to the grace mediated by her theological reflections. To do this, she must always embrace the prophetic role, else, her message falls short of the transformative effect it ought to have on those who hear it. This text will stand the test of time for its ability to engage and describe the effects of racism as a moral evil on human society. As one reads each page of this book, one begins to notice that the author has taken seriously the prophetic mandate. She does this skillfully by locating the discourse on racism within the boundaries of womanist theology. This approach is consistent with a biblical pattern; the prophets derive their calling to speak God's truth to society from their place at the margins. They experience with the poor and the outcasts the effects of injustice perpetuated by those at the helm of power. When they speak against oppression, it is against a moral evil they know in the real sense of the word. The same can be said of women and most especially of black women.

The text engages the lived experiences of blacks in western societies, especially societies founded and supported by black slave labor. With detailed research into the histories of such societies, the text unpacks the layers of oppressive narratives, social biases, immoral legal codes, and outright violence carried out against black persons by whites. Else one thinks that racism and violence against the bodies of blacks are simply social problems, the text shows how in western Christian intellectual tradition, a biased reading of some scriptural texts has been followed meticulously to validate oppression against blacks, and particularly black women. In a skillful manner, the text goes further to show how Hellenistic philosophical dualism has shaped the western Christian worldview in a way that violence against black bodies has become the norm in a two front approach; one religious, the other socio-cultural.

The text appropriates the narrative method familiar to womanist theology and black cultures to reflect on the experiences of black persons in western societies. The stories, experiences, and theologies of womanist theologians are given primacy as the text systematically offers a new vision for Christian theological anthropology that is truly ecumenical. The text invites white theologians to pay attention to theologies done at the margins for there is where new insights and pneumatic breakthroughs can be found to guide the stale and repetitious theologies currently being done by those at the center. Their failure to speak to the experiences of blacks is judged to be inexcusable.

This text has successfully reclaimed the voice of oppressed people and most particularly oppressed black women by paving the way for their experiences to be part of the content of theology today. If Christian theology is to be relevant in the third millennium, it must necessarily be truly inclusive in its content, vision, and methods. An inclusive reading of the ministry of Jesus Christ must necessarily be one that presents him as speaking against all structures of oppression; racism, xenophobia, sexism, poverty, violence and all other social vices.

This text is an important text that should become part of the required texts for college courses in liberation theologies, womanist and feminist theologies, Christian theological anthropology and courses that engage black experiences in western civilization. In a prophetic manner, this text can help to focus the discourse on race relations today in the United States. It can also be used as a guide for community discussions on what is fundamentally wrong with our social structures and the paths we can follow to remedy the problems.

    Dr. Simonmary Asese Aihiokhai
    Valparaiso University
    Valparaiso, Indiana

CHRONOLOGY OF BCTS ANNUAL MEETINGS

2016 Xavier University of Louisiana, New Orleans, Louisiana

2015 St. Norbert College, De Pere, Wisconsin

2014 Catholic Theological Union, Chicago, Illinois

2013 Bellarmine University, Louisville, Kentucky

2012 St. Thomas University, Miami Gardens, Florida

2011 Marquette University, Milwaukee, Wisconsin

2010 Stetson University, DeLand, Florida

2009 Atlanta University, Atlanta, Georgia

2008 Catholic Theological Union and Loyola University, Chicago, Illinois

2007 St. Meinrad Archabbey, St. Meinrad, Indiana

2006 Boston College, Boston, Massachusetts

2005 St. Mary's Seminary at the University of St. Thomas and St. Francis of Assisi Parish, Houston, Texas

2004 Xavier University, New Orleans, Louisiana

2003 Atlanta University, Atlanta, Georgia

2002 Gonzaga University, Spokane, Washington

2001 University of Dayton, Dayton, Ohio

2000 Marquette University, Milwaukee, Wisconsin

1999 University of Notre Dame, Notre Dame, Indiana

1998 Marquette University, Milwaukee, Wisconsin

1997 No meeting

1996   The University of San Diego, San Diego, California

1995   St. John University, New York, New York.
        Met in conjunction with ACHTUS (Academy of
        Hispanic Theologians in the United States)

1994   Mt. Vernon, Hotel, Baltimore, Maryland

1993   The Mexican American Cultural Center
        San Antonio, Texas

1992   Duquesne University, Pittsburgh, Pennsylvania

1991   The Atlanta University Complex, Atlanta, Georgia

1979   Second Meeting of the BCTS
        Motherhouse of the Oblate Sisters of Providence
        Baltimore, Maryland

1978   First Meeting of the BCTS
        Motherhouse of the Oblate Sisters of Providence
        Baltimore, Maryland

www.ingramcontent.com/pod-product-compliance
Lightning Source LLC
Chambersburg PA
CBHW042336150426
43195CB00001B/3